My Devoted Response

A Devotional Guide on Worship

Austin Ryan

Worship Catalyst Inc.

My Devoted Response: A Devotional Guide on Worship
Copyright © 2023 by Austin Ryan.
All rights reserved. Printed in the United States of America. No part of this book may be used or reproduced in any manner whatsoever without written permission except in the case of brief quotations embodied in critical articles or reviews.
For information contact;
Worship Catalyst
PO Box 758
Yulee, FL, 32034
www.worshipcatalyst.com
Cover design by Ben Lunn
Layout by Ben Lunn
Scripture quotations marked NIV are taken from the Holy Bible from the New International Version®. NIV®, Copyright © 1973, 1978, 1984, 2011 by Biblica Inc®. Used by permission of Zondervan. All rights reserved. Scripture quations marked NLT are taken from the Holy Bible from the New Living Translation, NLT, Copyright © 1996, 2004, 2007, 2013 by Tyndale House Foundation. Used by permission of Tyndale House Publishers Inc. Scripture quotations marked cev are taken from the Contemporary English Version. Copyright © 1991, 1992, 1995 by American Bible Society. Used by permission.
ISBN: 978-0-9967145-3-2

CONTENTS

Introduction   i
Week 1
Day 1: Worship is a Response   1
Day 2: God is Seeking Worshipers   5
Day 3: God Gets the Praise   9
Day 4: There is Power in Singing   13
Day 5: Pronouns in Worship   17
Days 6/7: Worship Like You're Not Alone   20

Week 2
Day 1: Worship is Sacrificial   24
Day 2: Expect Nothing Back   28
Day 3: Worship is Joyful   32
Day 4: Worshiping Through Pain   36
Day 5: Worship Can Be Unacceptable to God   41
Days 6/7: Worship is Something We Do Together   45

Week 3
Day 1: Through Jesus, For Jesus   48
Day 2: Satan Wants Worship   52
Day 3: Worship and Fear   57
Day 4: Thanksgiving and Awe   61
Day 5: Worship Should Never Be Rules-Based   66
Days 6/7: Chosen to Worship   70

Week 4
Day 1: Worship Requires Unity   74
Day 2: Repentance and Mission   78
Day 3: Worship and Temples   82
Day 4: Worship Should Often Be Loud   87
Day 5: God Doesn't Need Your Worship   91
Days 6/7: Keep Worshiping   95

Introduction

I've always been interested in cheerleaders.

Now before you take a preliminary stab at me, let me explain. When most people think about cheerleaders, they imagine a group of girls, and maybe one or two guys, all dressed the same. They wear skirts or really tight shorts (except for the guys, who wear embarrassingly tight pants). They typically have some sort of team-coordinated, colored top and wear white tennis shoes. They perform cheers, high kicks, and pom-pom shakes and they randomly throw people in the air. Many cheer teams wear bows in their hair—not small ones, but gigantic ribbons carefully mounted with perfect precision, and often twice the size of the girl's head.

This type of cheerleading isn't really what I'm talking about. In fact, you have just read the extent to my cheerleading knowledge. What I am talking about is the act of cheerleading—its function and desired outcome. Turns out cheerleaders are not just there to look good or to do really cool tricks like building body pyramids or flipping and flopping down an entire football field. Their primary job is—get this—to lead cheers. Like farmers or programmers or street sweepers, their name clearly defines their designated purpose. Cheerleaders are there to lead the crowd in getting pumped up by cheering and yelling.

I saw the Dallas Cowboys cheerleaders one time. I was twenty, and my friend Mike and I thought it would be a good idea to get tickets to the Cowboys home opener against the Washington Redskins. I'll never forget that day. We arrived early, found our end-zone seats, and then were immediately hungry because of the intoxicating smell you only get from the mixture of hot dogs, popcorn, and sixty thousand human bodies in a sports stadium. So, we spent

My Devoted Response

our meager life savings on food and sat back down. Pretty soon the cheerleaders showed up and started pumping up the crowd. They ran around, high kicked, and performed a routine to some Paula Abdul song. Once the fans were sufficiently loud, it was time for the players to emerge. Like gladiators headed into a coliseum, here came the Cowboys. We strained our heads to get a glimpse of the only three guys we had really come to see: Troy Aikman, Emmitt Smith, and Michael Irvin. These guys were the heroes. They were the ones who would lead the Cowboys to three Super Bowl wins in the next four years.

By mentioning the Cowboys, I realize I may have just alienated you as you now might be calling my sanity into question. So please feel free to substitute your favorite team and players. Maybe you like Pittsburgh and you want to imagine seeing old heroes like Ben Roethlisberger and Antonio Brown. Or maybe you're a northeasterner and you would be straining to see the heroes of the bygone New England Patriots Dynasty: Tom Brady and Rob Gronkowski. Maybe you're in D.C. and you love the Commanders. No heroes there (sorry!). You get the point. Of course, you might not watch American football. In that case, pick your favorite sports team and the heroes of that team and imagine them coming onto the field.

For us it was exhilarating. The Cowboys got the ball first and marched down to score on a twelve-yard run by Emmitt Smith. Pretty soon they were up by two touchdowns and never looked back. Every time they scored that day, which was a lot, the crowd went nuts. The sound was deafening, grown men were hugging each other, and beer was flying all over the place. I remember vividly the sights, sounds, smells, and feelings of that day. The only thing I can't remember seeing after the start of the game? The cheerleaders. Did they all disappear after their opening dance? Was their only job to get us fired up and then leave? No. They were there. Every time the Cowboys scored, they were doing their job: jumping, dancing, cheering, and leading us to do the same. The only thing is . . . we didn't need them. Nobody needed cues on when to stand and start hugging strangers. Nobody required direction on when to get louder to confuse the other team's offense. Nobody needed someone reminding them it was time to encourage the team on a tight 3rd and 1.

We just did it. We already knew what to do.

A few years later I arrived early for a morning worship service at a conference. I'm guessing there was a time-zone mix-up on my alarm because for me to arrive early in the morning at a conference would not be what I would call "normal." I was so early that the greeters weren't even there yet. I was so early that no preview music was playing. I was so early that the only person I saw over the next twenty minutes was a tech guy sleepily changing batteries on the stage microphones.

Since I had some extra time, I began to pray. It was a feeble prayer asking Jesus to connect with me. I told him that's what I needed. I asked Him to speak clearly to me and meet me in that place. It was really important that I somehow felt His presence within me and heard His voice about a specific decision I needed to make. I thanked Him for being so gracious and for giving me so many amazing things and people in my life. I spent time telling Him how I felt about Him and how humanity needs Him because of His love and patience and kindness that He always shows. Before long, I sensed a real connection to God, and He seemed to be answering my prayers. I can't describe this properly, but somehow, I knew what He was saying. A few minutes later I

My Devoted Response

was responding with a yes and thanking Him for clarity.

As this was going on, the room started to fill, the lights lowered, and I heard someone talk from the platform. He was probably wearing tight jeans and a scarf . . . in the summer. A keyboardist played a mellow string sound. Before long, the cheerleaders (worship leaders) had us standing, raising our hands, and singing. I remember my time with God that morning and the deep connection we had as I prayed, sang, and responded. But I don't remember much of anything about the cheerleaders. Turns out I didn't need them that day. I didn't need anybody prompting me to sing. I didn't need anybody giving me direction on what to think or feel. My focus wasn't on the cheerleaders; it was on the Hero.

How often do you experience God like that at church? When was the last time you forgot who was leading worship because you were so fixated on Jesus? Or do you rely on just the right song selection with just the right style of music at just the right volume to really connect with your Creator? If so, maybe you've forgotten—or never knew—what worship really is.

Cheerleaders are awesome. They are an important part of sports culture. Worship leaders are awesome. They play a critical role in leading people toward Jesus. But when someone like you, a true worshiper of a hero, or The Hero, really understands what you are cheering for, worship somehow starts to happen more frequently and automatically.

As a thirty-plus-year veteran of cheerleading—and by that I mean worship leading (and many of us do wear tight pants, but it's different)—the best experiences of worship take place when the people in the seats are fully engaged before they ever show up. When I meet people like that, I thank them because I can tell they understand a thing or two about what worship really is.

I want you to understand and experience God like that. When you do, you will have more energy and joy, peace and patience, faith and hope. You really will. You will approach your day with anticipation of the Hero, just as I did over football players at a Cowboys game—only more so and for better reasons! Church will be more engaging. And the best part? You won't just worship like that at church. You will experience this thing called worship every day of your life.

That's why I wrote this collection of devotions. This isn't just a devotional course for leaders or strong, spiritual types. It's for everybody—especially the people who make up the crowd, sitting in the seats. It's for you—wherever you are in your faith journey. I wrote this book because we all want to worship something more than just a football player or a lead singer. Deep within us, we long to experience the life that comes from real worship. To do that fully, we must first understand worship, specifically what the Bible says about it. So that is what we will do together. Each day we will look at some great passages all throughout God's word, along with a few modern stories. I would encourage you to spend the next four weeks, while you are going through this process, to turn off talk radio, country music, classic rock or whatever you listen to and listen to Christian music exclusively. I would even say to focus as much time as possible listening to worship songs specifically. This will be a great complement to this worship devotional experience. In the end, I pray this journey will give you a clearer understanding of this mysterious thing called worship, how we do it properly, and the God who deserves it.

A disclaimer: I've read some really heady, theologically deep books about the topic of worship written by seminary

My Devoted Response

professors who have spent their lives unpacking every small or large aspect of worship in a studious, college-level kind of way. This isn't one of those books. This is a simple guide that compiles and discusses some understandable, practical Scriptures that will give you a clearer view of what worshiping God can be like in your life and in your church. Each devotion is stand-alone and short. You can read them in any order and use them for group discussion or personal devotion.

As you read, I'm going to be your cheerleader, cheering you on so that you'll cheer on God and experience the thrill of being in His presence. But in the end, as you understand more and more about what the Bible says about worship, my goal is that you won't need me, or any other cheerleader, to worship God every single day of your life.

Week 1 - Day 1:
Worship Is a Response

On October 1, 2017, the city where I lived at the time, Las Vegas, suffered for eleven minutes under a barrage of gunfire from a single shooter who perched himself inside the Mandalay Bay hotel and shot relentlessly at innocent concertgoers across the street. Before it finally ended, fifty-eight citizens were killed and almost five hundred were injured. It was the largest mass shooting in the history of the United States.

I met people who were there that night and they described feeling like fish getting shot out of a barrel. They were defenseless in almost every way. Maybe you have tried to put yourself in the shoes of people in that situation or one like it. Would you run? Would you lie down? Would you find someone to lie on top of or under?

Out of instinct and fear, most people ran in hope of finding protection. But in a few instances, some people headed into the rain of bullets, risking their lives, to save whomever they could. I met one of those guys. His name is Joe. He was watching the concert when the gunfire began. He initially fled and got to a safe place. Then he turned around and went to help others who were not yet safe. He is a certified EMT and felt he needed to use his abilities to help others. One of the more intriguing stories from Las Vegas is of two sisters named Lulu and Lauren Farina who were attending the concert. Lauren had a bad knee and was in a wheelchair. When the shooting began, Lulu grabbed her and began dragging her to safety, but couldn't drag her sister

My Devoted Response

fast enough. Others were literally being gunned down all around them. Then seemingly out of the nowhere, one man, and then another, picked up Lauren and carried her to a safe place while Lulu ran beside them. Once Lauren and Lulu were safe, the two men left. As they were leaving, one of the guys left his flip-flops for Lauren because she had lost her shoes during the escape. This was a true act of heroism and beauty.

To Lauren and Lulu, these men were like angels. They wanted to thank them and give them a hug or take them out to eat or promise them a lifetime of servitude . . . who knows. They felt indebted to these guys for saving them. But the men were gone. Lauren and Lulu spent the next week posting pictures of the flip-flops on social media and sharing their story on local news, asking everyone who would listen to help them find the two mystery angels. Their natural response was to feel indebted to them for the rest of their lives, and at the very least to offer their sincere gratitude.

I'm not sure if they ever found these heroic men. If they did, I can imagine the tear-filled reunion the sisters would have experienced when they got a chance to thank these guys from the bottom of their hearts. You see, when someone does something profoundly good for your well-being, your unbridled, natural response is to thank them back in an equally profound way.

The Scripture:
"Sing for joy, O heavens! Rejoice, O earth! Burst into song, O mountains! For the Lord has comforted his people and will have compassion on them in their suffering."—Isaiah 49:13, NLT

Austin Ryan

What It Says About Worship:
In the previous verses of this passage, the Old Testament prophet Isaiah had just revealed to the Israelites that God was going to restore them from their future captivity in Babylon and cause them to become a nation again. This of course was amazing news! So, Isaiah couldn't help himself and he blurted out, "Sing for joy! Rejoice! Burst into song!" It was his natural and raw response to a good word from God. This, in its most organic form of our emotion, is worship.

God saves us. He heals us. He fixes something or renews something or answers a prayer and we can't help but say, "Yes! Thank You, God! I'm all Yours!" I think God loves it when we blurt out praise to Him. You see, worship is our devoted response to God for who He is and what He has done. We neither initiate it nor cause it. We are just responders to Someone who has saved our lives.

There's something in you and me that wants to say thanks. If someone saves your life or gives you something extraordinary, your innate desire is to give your life back to that person. This is natural. It's normal. It's not all that exceptional. In fact, in Romans 12, the apostle Paul called it reasonable. (We'll cover that Scripture in another session.)

Apply It:
Spend some time thinking about all God has already done for you: He's given you life, family, friends, food, home, hope . . . and through His Son, Jesus, He has saved you from certain destruction. As you reflect on all He is, blurt out how you feel about God. Don't hold back, just respond. And that response, in its truest, purest form, is worship.

My Devoted Response

Two Questions:
1. What ten things has God done for you that have saved or enriched your life? Take a moment and write them down.
2. What would be a proper way to say thanks for all God has done for you?

Week 1 - Day 2:
God is Seeking Worshippers

My dad, who has more than five decades of experience leading worship, has witnessed some really bad singers over the years. One woman, who happened to be one of the least-talented vocalists on planet Earth, joined his choir. All the members welcomed her with open arms. A new member had joined the growing choir and things were fun and jovial . . . until she started to sing.

The good thing about a choir is the more talented singers can cover up moderately untalented singers by sheer force. Unless of course, the force of a single untalented vocalist is so great that it crushes the combined strength of the moderately talented (and even the very talented.)

That is exactly what happened in the choir my dad was directing. This particularly bad singer was the worst kind. She was loud. Dad tried moving her around to different sections of the choir in hope of her learning a new part, or any part really. And all the time he prayed that somehow a certain squadron of the choir would be strong enough to once-and-for-all subdue and overcome her dreadful vocal chops.

They could not. The more she sang, the more confident she became, and the more the choir struggled to regain its once-solid sound.

One day, for no apparent reason, the woman went to Dad with an idea: "What if I recorded the parts around me so I can take it home, work on it, and more accurately sing the alto part of the song?" My dad was ecstatic and probably even purchased the small recorder for her so she could hear herself sing on tape, realize she was horrible, and reassign herself to another ministry in the church.

Oh, if things could be so easy. She recorded herself and the other altos, went home to listen, and then showed back to practice the next week.

"What did you learn from listening to yourself?" my dad asked.

Unfazed, the "singer" replied, "Here's what I learned: if I thought I really sounded in person as bad as I do on that tape, I would never sing again. I'm sure glad I don't!"

This story, and others, led me to design an audition process years ago. Since then, we have auditioned dozens of singers and musicians. Some have had great talent and great hearts. Many have had either talent or heart—or neither of them. As a leader, it is always challenging to suggest to a well-meaning, true-hearted person (like the woman in the story above) that God has given them amazing gifts . . . in something else.

Fortunately, God is never going to judge you on your ability to sing. He has either given you that talent or He hasn't. But there is a much more important audition of sorts—one we all must attend. And God is the only Judge. Jesus talked about this audition when He addressed a Samaritan woman in John 4. But this audition wasn't (and isn't) about vocal quality, but about how we worship. It's an audition of the heart and mind. And the prize is not just making it into a band. It's about gaining the very attention of God.

The Scripture:
"The time is coming—indeed it's here now—when true worshipers will worship the Father in spirit and in truth. The Father is looking for those who will worship him that way."—John 4:23, NLT

What It Says About Worship:
God is in white-hot pursuit of worshipers who worship in spirit and in truth. If God is seeking worshipers like this, we should understand what it means. To worship in spirit is to have a deep affection for God. To worship in truth is to worship Him for who He really is, not picking and choosing only His attributes and teachings with which we most agree. It also means that we live out what we say we believe. In Desiring God, John Piper described this idea of spirit and truth like this: "True worship comes from people who are deeply emotional and who love deep and sound doctrine. Strong affections for God rooted in truth are the bone and marrow of biblical worship."

God is actively looking for these kinds of worshipers. In my mind I see it like this: God is going from chair to chair in a church building while people are singing. He stands in front of each person one by one and listens—not to the sound of their voice, but to the sound of their heart. "Is he fully committed to Me?" "Does she really mean what she's singing?" "Does this person's life match up with those lyrics?"

The difference in God's audition process of your heart and a worship leader's audition process for new singers and players is this: You don't show up to an audition for God. It's all day, every day. He is listening to everything you say, do, and think from morning to night. I don't know about you, but I want God to slow down, linger, and relish more of my life. If that's going to be the case, I need to worship

Him completely and honestly, in spirit and in truth.

Apply It:
Acknowledge that God is with you right now. Tell Him that you want to live every moment for Him completely and honestly. Then try to remember throughout the day that God is listening and auditioning you as you live, speak, and think. Try setting an alarm on your phone that goes off every hour to remind you of His presence. At church, think through every lyric as you sing them. Be honest with God. Imagine Him standing in front of you listening, not to your voice, but to your heart. And live a great audition—fully worshiping in spirit and in truth.

Two Questions:
1. How is your "audition" going—the one where you worship daily in spirit and in truth?
2. If God is listening to everything you say and think from morning to night, what is He hearing?

Week 1 - Day 3:
God Gets the Praise

One Monday night in the fall, I'd invited a few guys to my house for a football-viewing party. We were in the backyard and talking while I was cooking up brats. One of my friends, we'll call him John, and I were discussing my house. My house is really nice, because my wife, Cami, has had a career in, and a serious love for, interior design. Everything is in its place, the furniture is good-looking, and everything goes together. It's the opposite of a bachelor pad. It's also the opposite of what it would look like if those decisions were up to me.

As I was turning the brats, John asked me about the house, what I spent on it, how long we'd owned it, and other quizzical questions like that. He said, "You know, Austin, you're in a good place in life." I asked him what he meant, and he talked about my family and my career, but I noticed he was more focused on the house. He told me that one day he would like to have a house as nice as mine.

You need to know one thing about John: he does not know Jesus. I wish he did. We've had many conversations about Him, but so far my friend has not chosen to follow. So here was an opportunity I had to say something about Jesus again. I could have said that Cami and I have followed God's principles financially most of our lives. I could have said that God had really blessed us beyond what we could have ever imagined. I could have said that God had given us some good breaks in the housing market. Instead, I said that we had owned three previous houses and we made

My Devoted Response

money on all of them and kept rolling the money into the next one so that now on our fourth home, we could have a bigger and nicer one.

No mention of God's favor. No mention of our diligent prayer to follow God's leadership in our lives in every aspect because He wants us to make good choices. I missed a "gimme" opportunity.

Compare that story with this next one. It happened while standing in line at the copy-making place at Office Max. I love that store. I don't know if it's the many varieties of pens, or the large sticky paper that goes on the wall so I can take notes at a meeting, or that fact that I can get really big stuff laminated. Whatever it is, I can walk around that store and never get bored. So, a few months after John and I had our house conversation, I was in line to get yet another thing laminated. I saw a customer at the counter looking at the printing job the "copy specialist" had just performed. He was looking at a large piece of nice paper. From my vantage point I could see it had military symbols and some words on it.

It caught my interest, so I approached the guy and asked him what it was. He told me it was a hymn for military veterans that he wrote. He invited me to read it. As I read, he continued talking, telling me why he wrote it, what it meant, and that he wrote the hymn in one sitting in about ten minutes. I was having a hard time listening to him and comprehending what I was reading at the same time, so I decided to act like I was reading so I could focus on what he was saying.

I looked up after what seemed like the right amount of time it would take someone to read this fairly long hymn and asked him if he had written anything else like this.

"No, I have never written anything before," he said. "God gave this to me. I'm not a writer. Only God could make this happen."

We were cut off by another copy specialist who was ready to assist me with my lamination, and I moved to that register. A few moments later I noticed the guy starting to leave so I caught his eye and said, "Congratulations on the hymn. I really appreciate your care for our veterans."

He was already moving toward the door, so he loudly replied, "God gave it to me! God gave it to me!" It was critical to this man that I understood there was a God and that He had inspired him to write this hymn. As he was saying this, my mind went back to the missed opportunity I had with John. My new hymn-writing friend was doing what I was not prepared to do—give God the glory He deserves. I'd missed an important opportunity to live out my worship.

The Scripture:
"Ascribe to the Lord the glory due his name."—Psalm 29:2, NIV

What It Says About Worship:
If God deserves something, make sure you give him credit for it. This was the flaw of my brat conversation with John. I ascribed to good financial choices and luck the glory that was due God's name. My Office Max, lamination-loving friend was not at all interested in receiving glory for the hymn he wrote. He made sure three times to ascribe the glory to God. The tragedy in my response to John's com-
about my house are two-fold. First, I missed an op-
ity to yet again show John that Jesus does care about

the details of our lives, and that He gives us good answers to hard questions if we will just ask, listen, and respond. But even worse was that I ascribed the glory to something else that belongs only to God. In other words, I gave worship to myself and my "luck" when I should have worshiped God. God is interested in us worshiping Him not just privately in prayer or through a quiet song, but outwardly, publicly, every day in conversations and real life.

Apply It:

If God has done something good, ascribe glory to His name around other people. Be clear. Be open. Be bold. Be honest. Has God done good things in your life? Tell someone. Don't be ashamed when you get a new car. Don't give glory to the low payment or "smoking good deal" you got. God provides all things, so honor and ascribe glory to His name. The car dealer isn't the hero; your "good sense" isn't either. God is! Church is not the only place we should mention how great Jesus is to us. Mention Him #IRL (in real life- if you are my age or older). In those moments, in non-church circumstances when you ascribe the Lord the glory due His name, God smiles because you are worshiping Him in spirit and in truth.

Two Questions:

1. What are five good things God has done in you, to you, for you, or through you?
2. What are two ways you can ascribe to God the glory for doing these things, especially in conversation with other people?

Week 1 - Day 4:
There is Power in Singing

Have you ever been in jail? Or perhaps you know someone who has? I haven't, but I've watched enough of those television reality shows to know it's not a place I'd like to spend a lot of time. It's stark and sterile. Cold looking. Nothing welcomes the person with a sense of hominess. Staring at those bare walls all day surely gives the incarcerated person time to think a lot about what he or she has done and what changes they will make when they are released.

What kind of emotions do you think you would have if you were arrested and put in prison? You might feel embarrassed, frustrated, sad, or angry for getting caught. What if you were in trouble for doing something right? Maybe you helped someone finish their taxes or baited a hook for a young kid or paid for someone else's food at a restaurant—and some authority figure thought your actions were completely out of bounds and threw you in jail, away from your family, your friends, and your life? Would you be angry? Confused? Irritated? Scared?

Let's add one more layer. What if they beat you until you were bloody and bruised just before they threw you in the jail?

Now how do you feel? What would you do? Would the fetal position be in order? Maybe you're a screamer. Is desperation a good way to describe it?

My Devoted Response

This is what happened to Paul and Silas in Acts 16. They did a good thing, but got arrested, beaten, and thrown in jail under the watchful eye of a guard. They had every right to be resentful and scared. So, they did what any normal, rational person would do in that situation, right? They started praying and singing hymns.

Excuse me?

Yeah, they began to sing. Out loud. We don't know which hymns. Is there one called, "Lord, Get Me Out of Here?" or "Um, What Just Happened?" Those would be the hymns I would sing if I even considered singing at all, which probably wouldn't be one of my first one hundred natural responses in that situation.

"Hey, Buddy. I'm losing a lot of blood over here from where that guard beat me and am feeling like I might faint. I don't know when we're getting out of here, but it seems like the perfect time for us to execute a stirring anthem!"

It just doesn't make any sense. But they sang. And when they sang, something crazy happened.

The Scripture:
"About midnight Paul and Silas were praying and singing hymns to God, and the other prisoners were listening to them. Suddenly there was such a violent earthquake that the foundations of the prison were shaken. At once all the prison doors flew open, and everyone's chains came loose." Acts 16:25-26, NIV

What It Says About Worship:
There is power in singing. And it is a choice. I can ima ine that Paul and Silas might have been scared, frustra

irritated, confused. But at some point, in the silence and darkness of the cell, one of them made the decision to kick off a verse of their favorite song—honoring and committing their lives to Jesus. They looked past their circumstances and began to praise. I am sure they still had some non-joyful feelings as they worshiped, but just the act of singing turned out to be a powerful thing.

Your hard time might not be a literal prison. Or maybe it's a relational one—a challenging marriage or another relationship. Maybe it's a parental one—your kids are making unhealthy choices. Maybe you're almost out of money. Maybe you're addicted to something that is slowly destroying you, or you have a health issue you can't control. Maybe you feel like nobody cares. Maybe you hate your job and your future and your life. Any of these can feel like prison. You are stuck and frustrated or lonely or angry or sad. You have some prison bars keeping you cemented in place, and you have a guard making sure you don't escape.

The decision you make at this point is important. Do you force the bars open with your strong will? Do you keep fighting the system? Do you throw your hands up and simply let things play out however they are going to play out? These are all reasonable choices for most people.

But you aren't most people. You are a worshiper.

Apply It:
Sing. The next time you feel yourself behind the bars of your prison cell, pick a song, any key, turn on the radio, get in the shower, go on a drive—whatever makes you feel more comfortable—and belt out a song of praise to God. Tomorrow, do it again. And the next day, do it again. Then go to church this weekend and sing the songs there. In the

My Devoted Response

darkest times and places in your life, sing a song to God. And while you sing, look for Jesus. He's just around the next chorus. He's in the lyrics of the second verse. He's listening carefully and His hands are on the prison bars that are holding you in, ready to rip them off their hinges.

Don't doubt. Believe.

Don't worry. Worship.

Don't fear. Sing.

There's power in a song. But in order to receive that power, you've got to sing it.

Two Questions:
1. What "prisons" do you find yourself in these days? They could be physical, emotional, relational, etc.
2. In what ways can you incorporate singing to God as a consistent part of your life?

Week 1 - Day 5: Pronouns in Worship

When I was growing up, my family and I were kind of English language snobs. Not with all things. We still said things like, "We're fixin' to go to the store" and "Whatcha doin'?" That ain't good English. But at least we knew it wasn't good English and why it wasn't. We were actually cool about it, except for one area.

When it came to prepositions, specifically not ending a sentence in one, we were the kind of family about whom others would get irritated. If you were hanging around us and said, "Where's your mom at?" We would reply with a cocky, "I don't know, where was she going to?" If you didn't catch on to this egotistical preposition game, we might even amp it up with an even more ridiculous, "To where was she going at?" Having understood that we were then better than you because of our amazing handling of this one English language rule, you would leave the situation feeling defeated, while we would cheer ourselves on as the kings and queens of preposition management.

We tended also to cringe at the pronoun missteps into which our culture has fallen. Using plural pronouns when we should use singular ones. "The person checked their rearview mirror to see if they were being followed." Ugh. Using the proper pronoun is important!

To whom am I writing this book? Myself? You? Someone sitting next to you? Of course, I'm writing this book to you.

How do you know that? Pronouns. If I were writing this book to someone sitting next to you, I would keep writing things like, "The person next to you should quit ending sentences in prepositions. He (or she) is nice and all, but he (or she) doesn't sound smart."

In the normal flow of our conversational lives we pay close attention to pronouns, and we probably don't even realize it. How weird would it be for me to look at another person in the room, but call you by name and talk to you directly? You would think I was crazy and say, "Who are you talking to?" And I would say, "To whom am I talking?" And you would punch me in the throat.

As it is important to recognize pronouns in life, it is also important to recognize them in the songs we sing at church. Some songs give us lyrics that help us sing things about God and others give us lyrics that help us sing words directly to Him. Noticing the difference can enhance your worship experience immediately.

The Scripture:
"I will sing of your love and justice, Lord. I will praise you with songs."—Psalm 101:1, NLT

What It Says About Worship:
The psalmist, David, did in this psalm what he wrote over and over in his writing. Ignoring any human audience, he put his full and complete attention on God. "I will sing of your love and justice, Lord. I will praise you with songs." We're in the room watching David and God, but it isn't about us. It's just about David and his complete focus toward his Creator. He might have had his eyes closed as he recited this song. He might have been looking heaven- But for sure, he was not looking at you or me.

He was intentionally talking or singing directly to God and God alone.

Apply It:
Next Sunday at church when you sing, focus on the pronouns in the songs. Is the song about God or is it to God? If it is to God, put your complete focus on Him and sing it to Him. It's just like you're talking to a friend. You are eye-to-eye and heart-to-heart. Don't look around. Don't focus on other people in the room. Don't think about what other people are saying or singing to God. This isn't about them. This is about you and your direct dialogue with Jesus. Plus, it's creepy when you sing songs to God and make eye contact with other people. On the other hand, if the pronouns are third person, singing about God (He, Him), make eye contact with the worship leaders on stage, glance at the person with whom you came to church or give a high five to the stranger sitting next to you. Is that weird? It is exactly what we do at football games when we say good things about the guy who just scored. Try it.

So, focus on the pronouns and always remember to whom or about whom you're singing at.

Three Questions:
1. What is one of your favorite worship songs or hymns? Is it a song that you mostly sing to God or mostly sung about God?
2. When singing a song to God at church, are you sometimes distracted by the people around you? What are some ways you could tune out people and things around you and sing the songs directly to God?
3. When singing songs about God at church, how might you engage with others around you as you worship together?

My Devoted Response

Week 1 - Days 6 and 7: Worship Like You're Not Alone... Because You're Not

My mom used to say this really creepy statement to me on occasion: "Someone is always watching you." The more you whisper when you say it, the creepier it gets. Imagine staring into the eyes of a ten-year-old kid and whispering that. The once self-assured boy is now looking behind his back all the time assuming someone is hiding in the bushes with a video camera or, worse, is about to jump out and get him.

Now, these days, whether you know it or not, or like it or not, you're probably being recorded most of the time. It's hard to get away from video surveillance or someone's cell phone. But that isn't what Mom was talking about. She was saying that someone is always watching you as you go through life, not because they want to attack you or blackmail you, but because they want to learn from you. This is a less creepy take on the phrase, but potentially more challenging. The way we talk, act, walk, serve, lead, and even sing is always under surveillance by someone.

With that in mind, I have a certain family member who loves Jesus with all his heart and has spent a lifetime serving Him in various ways through his local church and beyond. Any pastor would look at this guy as a model church member and Christian. There's only one issue: he doesn't like singing in church.

It's not that he doesn't like other people singing in church—he's very complimentary of others' talents and abilities. But when it comes to opening his mouth and singing out loud where others can hear, that's not in his wheelhouse. You can forget about swaying or raising a hand partially up to the sky.

Lots of people are like that because singing seems weird. I get it. Where in today's culture, except for the seventh inning stretch of baseball games and in Irish pubs, do you stand together with a bunch of other sane adults and sing? It's rare. But at church we are expected to stand and sing out loud. People who struggle with this, these "non-singing" types, also tend to have stoic faces when church songs are being sung. They are very serious. Don't smile! Don't show emotion! Don't. Move. A. Muscle!

As they stand there, not singing, not moving, not emoting in any way, people are watching. Someone is always watching. And as they observe you in action, or in your lack of action, what are they learning about Jesus? Do they figure that He must be amazing because His followers can't help but sing loudly to Him? Do they imagine Him to be boring because His followers yawn in His presence? Do they assume He is a taskmaster because His followers seem to be there out of coercion?

Someone is always watching you . . . even when you are at church.

The Scripture:
"He put a new song in my mouth, a hymn of praise to our God. Many will see and fear the Lord and put their trust in him."—Psalm 40:3, NIV

My Devoted Response
What It Says About Worship:
There is a connection between your singing to God and other people putting their trust in Him. People are watching you. Don't worry too much, they're not really listening to the quality of your voice, but they are paying close attention to the fervency of your worship. Now, you might be like my relative and not enjoy singing, or maybe you don't have the physical capacity to sing because of an ailment. Then think through how you can still be engaged in a fervent conversation with God, even physically, while others around you are singing. What would your facial expression or body posture be like if you were expressing your undying love and devotion to someone who saved your life? Obviously, God is our primary audience of our praise, but people are watching too, and the impact of your expression, or lack of expression, might be more than you have ever considered.

I have spent a good deal of my ministry life in churches where a lot of people were not yet followers of Jesus. I would often tell the Christians in the room that the far-from-God people were not looking at how I, as the leader, sang to God; I was getting paid to sing with passion. Instead, they were paying close attention to them, the attenders.

People will come to our services, wondering, Is this God real? Do people really believe this stuff? If God is real, do His followers really think He is awesome? This psalm spells out a reality we must consider as worshipers: the fervency with which we express our devotion to God influences how nonbelievers view God. And for many it will even impact whether they decide to put their trust in Him.

Apply It:
Sing. Sing loudly. Sing passionately at church every week and on every song. On songs you sing to God, make sure you are putting your full attention and affection toward Him. On songs you sing about God, sing to convince others the lyrics are true. Sing them with all your heart and let everyone around you know that without question, this God is worthy of your entire life, including your voice.

Two Questions:
1. If someone who did not know Jesus watched you respond to Him in a church service, would they be convinced He is worth following?
2. Who is watching you? List two or three people who might be determining how they view Jesus based on your worship of Him. If you have children, you can start there. They are definitely watching you worship.

Week 2 - Day 1: Worship Is Sacrificial

There are a few statements nobody ever wants to hear:

"The pathology report is back. We need to talk."

"This is the county jail. Are you the parent of John Smith?"

And in a different way, but similarly chilling, "I'm moving to a new house on Saturday. Can you help me with my stuff?"

I got that last call, or text actually, a few years ago from a guy moving to our city. I had met him a few times when he visited, but this was not a close friend by any means.

I do appreciate alarming information coming by text instead of phone calls. It gives me time to process. People always know when you're lying on the phone. "Uh, yeah . . . about Saturday. I have a . . . I need to check with my wife first because, you know, she holds the calendar and all. And our daughter has a thing on the other side of town and . . . well, I just don't know what time it starts or what day it is or if she's even involved in it, really. So let me get back to you. I've got your number and I'll dial it and give you an answer when I get all of this sorted out." Everybody knows you're lying when your phone response sounds like that.

But texting is different. First, you can be careful not to open it when you read the first preview line. That way you have plausible deniability when they ask about your non-response two weeks later. "You moved? You should have asked me to help! You did? Oh man, I don't think I got that text. Let me check. . . . Wow! Yeah, there it is! I just somehow didn't see it when it came in or something. Weird. It must have come in late. My phone has been acting weird lately. Sorry about that. I would have loved to help! I love moving washers and dryers up to third-floor apartments. Call me next time you move, for sure."

Also, when someone texts, you can take some time to think and formulate a caring note that sounds somewhat credible. "Hey John! Man, I would love to help you, but I already promised my grandmother I would see her in the nursing home on Saturday. She has been looking forward to it and I would hate to disappoint the matriarch of our family. She turns ninety-five next month and I'm not sure how many more Saturdays I have to spend with her. Hit me up next time, for sure!"

So, my family showed up to help this guy move. I wasn't looking forward to it. It was easy to find his new house because in the driveway sat the largest U-Haul truck in the universe. We headed into the new house to find fifteen other people I knew who had responded with a yes to his text for help. They had already started unloading boxes, lamps, furniture pieces, and sporting equipment. We all jumped in to help and within about forty-five minutes the truck was empty, and all their stuff was in the proper room.

As we were leaving it hit me, getting off the couch, getting in the car, and driving to this guy's house to help him move felt like a huge sacrifice. Moving is hard and dirty work—especially in Las Vegas in the summer. But in the end, I was glad we had gone. Strangely, it felt good to sacrifice. It felt even better to sacrifice together with my family and the others. And it felt best knowing I had done something that made a real difference in a family's life.

The Scripture:
"Let us offer through Jesus a continual sacrifice of praise to God, proclaiming our allegiance to his name. And don't forget to do good and to share with those in need. These are the sacrifices that please God."—Hebrews 13:15-16, NLT

What It Says About Worship:
Sacrifice pleases God and worship is sacrificial. I'm not sure worship was ever meant to be clean and tidy, easy or "fun." If you think back to Exodus and Leviticus where God set up a system of sacrifice, whereby we worship Him and He atones for our sin; it included blood. Lots of it. Bulls, heifers, lambs, birds, rams, and more. The owners of the animals sacrificed food, money, and even companionship to worship God. It wasn't as easy as pulling up to the Temple and singing a few songs at the early service so they could make it to the game in time. It cost something!

Paul affirmed this concept in Romans 12:1 where he wrote that offering our bodies as a living sacrifice is our reasonable act of worship. I have often wondered why Paul went to the trouble of writing the word living before sacrifice. Here is my conclusion: Had he simply said, "Offer your bodies as a sacrifice," the readers might have assumed him to mean some sort of mass suicide. Their only real concept of sacrifice was full devotion, to the point of death. The new believers in Paul's day might be disheartened by our lack of sacrifice and need for stylized preference when it comes to worship. True worship means we are sacr something: time, preference, money, energy, etc.

Apply It:
Let us proclaim our allegiance to Jesus' name sacrificially. Give something up. That style. That time. That sleep. That money. That privacy. Offer up to God a sacrifice of praise. Sometimes it will be by singing a song, even one you don't like. Sometimes it will be through giving food to someone in need when it means you won't get to eat anything yourself. Sometimes it will be by waking up early to pray and read the Bible when you went to bed only four hours before. Sometimes it will be by giving up a Saturday to help someone move. In every case, worship is meant to be sacrificial. And when it is, God is pleased.

Two Questions:
1. What are you sacrificing to worship Jesus?
2. As you pray, what do you sense God might be calling you to sacrifice to worship Him more fully?

Week 2 - Day 2: Expect Nothing Back

I have this longtime friend named Nancy. She is an RN. This came in handy one day when her next-door neighbor called her frantically saying that her husband wasn't breathing. Nancy and her husband, Ron, took off next door, barefooted, leaving the front door open. Their neighbor was standing by her door waiting for them. She escorted them to the master bedroom where the man lay, not breathing, still on his bed. His skin had already turned blue.

Nancy told Ron to grab the man's upper body while she grabbed his feet. They moved him to the floor where Nancy started CPR. The wife called 9-1-1 and waited for what would be the longest ten minutes of her life—and Nancy's.

Nancy continued chest compressions and provided breath into his mouth in perfect steady rhythm. She talked to him, urging him to fight for life, not really knowing if he could hear her or not. For all practical purposes, her neighbor was dead.

Finally, the paramedics arrived with a defibrillator, and after several tries got his heart working again. Miraculously, a few days later, the man returned home and continued his life.

As Nancy told me this story, my biggest question didn't have to do with the CPR or her neighbor's heart condition leading up to and following this event. My biggest question was about his response to Nancy days and weeks later.

How thankful was this man? She'd literally saved his life. He was dead, and she kept him going until he could be revived. Surely, he had tried to think of multiple ways to say thank you. After all, Nancy gave him more years to his life; years to spend with kids and grandkids. Years to travel with his spouse. Years to build genuine relationships with friends, watch sunsets, and eat Chick-fil-A. So how did he say thanks? Nancy laughed, almost embarrassed, and said he had been showering her and Ron with thanks, gift cards, meals, and more. It made sense. How could you say thanks to someone who moved you from death to life? The only realistic gift is a lifetime of servitude. But Nancy would never accept that. She didn't even want the gift card.

The Scripture:
"Accept my freewill offerings of praise, O Lord, and teach me your rules."—Psalm 119:108, ESV

What It Says About Worship:
Nancy's story is a modern-day metaphor for what Jesus did for us. We were the ones lying on the bed lifeless, and He came and took us from death to life. Remember, we were not brought from sickness to health. We were dead in our transgressions and sins and then Jesus made us alive (Ephesians 2:5). Our natural response is to give an offering of praise to our Savior. And in this psalm, we see that our offering is a freewill one. This means simply that we offer our praise response to God expecting nothing in return. Often, we praise God by tithing, going to church, doing nice things, and generally living right, expecting all along the way that God will respond to our goodness by doing good things for us. We will get the better job, the raise, the health, the decent kids, the simpler life. But remember something: you were dead. Jesus brought you back to life.

My Devoted Response

You respond with your own life lived for Him. He doesn't owe you anything.

How preposterous would it be for Nancy's next-door neighbor to give her a gift card to some fancy steak house and then come by the next day expecting her now to give him something nice. "Come on, Nancy. I gave you a steak dinner. Surely you have something nice to give me." Knowing Nancy, she probably would. Knowing Jesus, He does. But our response of praise to Him is not with the condition that we get something back from Him. He already did His part by saving us.

Apply It:
It's interesting that the psalmist did ask for two things as he offered up his freewill offering. First, he asked for God to accept the offering. It was important to Nancy's neighbor that she accept the gifts he offered. It was important to the psalmist that God accept his worship. Second, he asked for God to teach him His rules. The psalmist offered up his life as a freewill offering to God, expecting nothing in return, except to learn more about the rules of God so he could live even more specifically by them.

His ask of God was to show him how to give every last part of himself to his Creator. Follow this pattern. Give yourself completely to God today through prayer and through living. Expect nothing in return. But ask God to be even clearer with you about how you can live for Him completely, holding nothing back. Then your life will be offered as a freewill praise to God. And He will receive it.

Two Questions:

1. What nice thing has someone done for you? How did you say thanks?

2. In what ways can you say thanks to God in response to Him bringing you from death to life?

Week 2 - Day 3: Worship is Joyful

The President of the United States was being called to account for some potentially shady dealings with another country. The ice caps were melting at a much faster rate than ever anticipated and soon we would no longer have a place called Miami. A gunman walked into a church in Brazil and killed five people and wounded countless more. In Sudan the government was killing its own people, many of them children. Stocks were on the decline, and experts suggested we consider hiding money under our mattresses.

You might consider all of this to be a year of bad news. But in fact, each of these stories were part of one single day's reporting on a popular news website. After perusing the web pages and reading all this bad news, I found it difficult not to feel helpless, sad, afraid, and even joyless. The world around us was crumbling, and it still is. Evil people seem to be getting eviler. Dictators seem to be getting more ruthless. Finances seem to be getting tighter.

Perhaps you could point to some bad news in your own life. Your financial situation is dire, or your physical health is fading, or you have a relationship that won't heal, or you have recently experienced a deep loss. In each scenario you might find yourself helpless, sad, afraid, or joyless. If you are, you're not alone. According to the 2018 World Happiness Report, only 33 percent of Americans considered themselves happy. The global happiness leader was the people of Finland. They scored a 7.6 out of a 10 on the happiness scale. In fact, eight out of the top ten countries were cold-weather countries. (I wonder if they are happier because they never have to see themselves in a swimsuit.)

If you are experiencing personal bad news and that is coupled with dwelling on the national and global bad news, you might struggle to imagine how you could live with joy. And yet, the life of a Jesus follower is characterized by joy (see Galatians 5:22). In fact, we can joyfully worship God, no matter what our circumstances.

The Scripture:
"When anxiety was great within me, your consolation brought me joy."—Psalm 94:19, NIV
"Come, let us sing to the Lord! Let us shout joyfully to the Rock of our salvation."—Psalm 95:1, NLT
"Let all that I am praise the Lord; may I never forget the good things he does for me."—Psalm 103:2, NLT

What It Says About Worship:
Worship with joy! The psalmist is giving us a clear directive: when you worship God, come to Him with great joy, even shouting as you come!

Pretty simple, right? But isn't there all kinds of bad news around us? How can we experience real joy?
We are not asking how we can act joyful or put on a happy face. The song "Don't Worry, Be Happy" is fun and all, but it provides no pathway to joy. In these psalms, the psalmist gives an important clue to how he was able to worship joyfully—even amid the darkest times.

must realize that joy comes from God. We can't
 . We can't smile through the pain and force joy
 ringing from us. Joy is from God. The psalmist,

My Devoted Response

as he wrote Psalm 94, was experiencing this joy from God. I am sure that this psalmist had a lot of reasons not to have joy, just like you and me. We can easily assume that he had some degree of difficulties in his life—family issues, tough decisions, or illness. He specifically mentioned his personal struggle with anxiety. But even still, as he wrote this worship song, he started it with, "When my anxiety was great within me, your consolation brought me joy." He worshiped with joy, and even reasoned that we should do so in the next psalm, 95, not because life was all rainbows and unicorns, but because God is available and ready to give us joy.

To worship joyfully, we must realize that joy comes from God.

Second, we must resist trying to find joy from other sources. We worship things in which we try to find joy. If I find try to find joy in a smartphone, I worship it. If I try to find joy in a new car, I worship it. If I try to find joy in a spouse or a child, I worship them. It's not that God doesn't sometimes provide joy to us through these and other things. He often does. But we must remember that the source of that joy is God. If we go looking for joy in money or people, health, or things, we will always be let down because these things all fade.

Finally, as David wrote in Psalm 103:2, the goodness of God is a key component to both having joy and worshiping God with joy. After stating this discipline of never forgetting the good things God does, David uses the rest of the psalm to list at least twenty things that God had done either in David's life or for all of humanity. This practice of focusing on the good things God has done in our lives is a key component and the third step in finding joy.

Apply It:
Stop looking for joy in new shiny things. Hold off on buying the thing that you believe might fill the joy void in your life. And if you have been joyless because of a person in your life who is not living up to their end of the relationship, ask God if He will help you untie yourself from trying to get the joy for your life from him or her. Remember, that person is not the source of joy. God is.

Finally, ask God to remind you of all the good things you have in life. Then, like King David did, write them down. Fill a page with names of friends and mentors, moments when you were encouraged, things you possess, lives you have touched, situations that have led you to where you are today, churches that have invested in you, and many other things. As you start writing you will begin to see God's activity in your life through the good days and the bad.

Realize where joy comes from. Resist trying to find joy from other sources. Remember what God has already done. And then joy, like a trickle and then hopefully a flood, will invade your life. No matter your circumstance or how much bad news you might experience, you will be able to truly worship with joy, the One who has given you all that joy in the first place.

Two Questions:
1. What are the things, other than God, in which you have tried to find joy?
2. Can you, like King David, think of twenty great things about God? These can be either his characteristics, or things He has done for you directly. If so, get to work writing them down.

Week 2 - Day 4: Worshiping Though Pain

Living on the Gulf coast of the United States for almost a decade, I saw my share of hurricanes and tropical storms. Everyone in its path must prepare by boarding up windows, buying extra water bottles, and making tough decisions about whether to leave town—and all their possessions. Everyone with the Weather Channel has seen the devastation big storms can bring: downed houses, flooded cars, eroded beaches.

As these storms move inland and eventually reveal their damage, no matter how many structures they destroy, they never seem to destroy one thing: palm trees.

Imagine being a palm tree. You are hanging out, minding your own business, and making killer coconuts when out of the blue comes a wind that starts small and increases to more than 100 miles per hour. All around buildings crumble, cars wash by, and the beach holding your roots starts to erode. You give a confident look to your fellow palms who, like you, are bending way over but not breaking or falling. How is that possible? How could you possibly survive a multiple-hour onslaught?

Some of it has to do with your ability to bend. Many trees aren't as flexible, so they snap or rip out of the ground. Some of it has to do with how old you are. Mature trees are better able to withstand storms. And some of it has to do with your root system. Your roots don't grow that deep, but they grow sideways and connect with other roots from other palm trees creating a strong wall that is difficult to knock over.

Why am I talking about trees and what makes them strong? And why do I keep referring to you as a tree? Here's why: you want to be a big, strong tree that can withstand unexpected hurricane-forced winds, such as sudden deaths in the family, broken relationships, wayward children, abuse, or illness. The question is not if the wind is going to pick up and try to knock you down. The question is how will you respond when it does?

The Scripture:
"At this, Job got up and tore his robe and shaved his head. Then he fell to the ground in worship and said, 'Naked I came from my mother's womb, and naked I will depart. The Lord gave and the Lord has taken away; may the name of the Lord be praised.'"—Job 1:20-21, NIV

What It Says About Worship:
Job was a wealthy landowner. He had lots of animals and kids and was a well-respected member of his region. Most notably, Job loved God with all his heart. One day, the wind started blowing: his animals were stolen, his servants were murdered, one of his houses was destroyed in a windstorm, and his sons and daughters died when the house collapsed on them. He received this news all in a matter of minutes.

Before he came up with a plan to solve the problem, before he even considered what he was supposed to feel in a moment like this, Job did something amazing. He worshiped God. Don't think for a second that the Bible glosses over sadness and pain. It does not.

My Devoted Response

Job did what people in those days did when they were completely broken, grieved, and defeated. He tore his clothes, shaved his head, and laid in the dirt. He wasn't trying to send a team of people to fight off the raiders who had stolen his animals or murdered his servants. He didn't send a servant to double check on his kids.

He didn't even organize a prayer meeting to ask God for help. He just fell on his face and stopped everything to grieve. And in his grief, he started talking.

"Naked I came from my mother's womb," he said, "and naked I will depart." Perspective. God didn't owe Job anything. He wanted to make sure he said that out loud. "The Lord gave, and the Lord has taken away." It was God who gave Job everything that was taken from him. Job had just been a steward. As he reminded himself out loud, he finished his statement with an acknowledgment that even though a great tragedy had happened, God was still worthy of praise: "May the name of the Lord be praised."

How could someone experience such grief with such a worshipful heart? Was he faking it? How could he worship if he hadn't even processed the loss? I think the answer is in the palm tree. When a strong wind comes unexpectedly and threatens to destroy it, it doesn't snap in half or get yanked up by the roots. Instead, it leans into its maturity. Hebrews 6:1 mentions it this way: "Let us move beyond the elementary teachings about Christ and be taken forward to maturity" (NIV). Small Christians are like small trees—they can't stand the wind. But mature Christians are like mature trees—they withstand storms and get stronger. In fact, the tragedy both requires and develops maturity.

There is also this issue of the roots. Palm trees aren't that strong on their own, but when their roots join with other palms' roots, they all get stronger. We need spiritual roots that grow and expand to other people so we can make it through tragedy together.

Job realized that if he was going to make it through the grief, he was going to need the presence of God. Bad things happen. When they do, we have two choices: Go through the grief with God or go through the grief without God. It's simple.

So, Job's world fell apart. But he was mature. His love for God was unflappable. He had perspective, realizing that God gave him everything and had every right to take it away. And because of perspective, and the steady progression of growing as a follower of God, the huge wind that erupted in his life could not shake his faith. Instead of blowing him away from God, it blew him to God. He didn't think about it or process it. He just did what he knew how to do. He worshiped.

Apply It:
Make maturing in Christ a priority. Pray daily. Read God's Word and reflect on it. Be accountable to someone for your actions and thoughts. Go to church every week. The winds are going to blow again. What will be your immediate and natural response? Will you be angry with God? Will you run away from Him? Or will you worship Him through the pain? If you, like Job, can come to a place of worship, you can have something he hoped for more than anything else-a lifetime of God's presence.

My Devoted Response

Four Questions:

1. What is the worst thing you have had to go through?
2. What were some of your immediate thoughts and feelings?
3. If something tragic happened to you or a family member today, do you think you would be able to have Job's response?
4. What are some next things you need to do to grow in maturity as a follower of Christ?

Week 2 - Day 5:
Worship Can Be Unacceptable to God

This has happened to everyone: Your family is in the car driving somewhere and everything is going great. Then out of the blue, you inhale through your nose and catch the faint whiff of something unpleasant. Is there something outside? Maybe an oil well. Or some old food that got stuck between the seats. Surely, it's that.

Because you are now in investigative mode, you take a longer and more dramatic sniff . . . or maybe a few smaller, quicker ones, so you can get to the bottom of the increasingly off-putting odor.

This time the smell is really strong and bad, and over the past ten seconds has changed from a slight inconvenience to a full-frontal assault on all things decent. Your mind is now fully engaged in this smell. Do you start blaming people first or roll down the window to double check that it's not outside and let in some fresh air? If it is from the outside, you don't want to roll down the window and bring more of it inside. How do you decide? So, you start blaming people. Kids first . . . or Dad, depending on how things usually go in your family. Mom almost never gets blamed for this for some reason. If you have guests in the car, especially if they are not close friends or if they are older, it gets even more confusing, because you don't want to blame them or even acknowledge it.

Maybe the others don't smell it. But of course they smell

it. How could they not? It's like suddenly someone threw a squirrel that's been dead three days, in between the front row and the back. Now you start to imagine how you might apologize to the guests about your disgusting family. But then it hits you that maybe it was one of them and you don't want everyone with your last name to vehemently deny it leaving only your friends to blame. So, you finally decide to act like it never happened. Eventually the cloud will clear. Hopefully the kids won't start laughing.

That nightmare, lived out probably a million times a day, almost always ends in laughter, especially for younger kids.

Eventually somebody can't hold back any longer and they start to snicker. Then everybody else joins in. Bad smells are often entertaining, depending on what they are, and sometimes they are a riot! But there is another kind of bad smell that's not nearly as funny.

The Scripture:
"I hate, I despise your religious festivals; your assemblies are a stench to me. Even though you bring me burnt offerings and grain offerings, I will not accept them. Though you bring choice fellowship offerings, I will have no regard for them. Away with the noise of your songs! I will not listen to the music of your harps."—Amos 5:21-23, NIV

What It Says About Worship:
God doesn't listen to our songs just because we show up and sing them. We sometimes should probably keep our mouths shut rather than sing. Could our singing actually be a burden to God? It was God Himself who said to the Israelites, "Your New Moon feasts and your appointed festivals I hate with all my being. They have become a burden to me; I am weary of bearing them" (Isaiah 1:14, NIV). And

in the verse before that He says, "Stop bringing meaningless offerings! . . . I cannot bear your worthless assemblies" (NIV).

What was going on among the Israelites that God chose to stop listening to their worship? How could worship deteriorate from being a beautiful thing to becoming a noxious smell coming from the back row of the minivan? For the Israelites they were living lives Sunday through Friday that did not look a whole lot like the "worship" they were offering at the Temple on Saturdays. They were disobedient to God. They were taking advantage of people. They did not feed the poor. They were always looking out for themselves more than others. They even chose other gods if God didn't live up to their expectations.

At their religious services they were praying, giving money, singing, listening to a message—following the script. But God knew they were not interested in living a life that was fully devoted to Him only. There was nothing wrong with their worship form, but their hearts were far from God.

Now that we understand the formula, how can we continue to produce worship experiences that are noxious to God? We can live lives Monday through Saturday that don't match up to the words we sing on Sunday. We can be disobedient to His Word. We can take advantage of people. We can choose not to feed the poor. We can look out for ourselves more than others. We can adopt other gods: money, television, sports, popularity, etc. If some or all these things are true in your life, your worship is unacceptable. It's meaningless. It's wasted. And it is a burden to God.

My Devoted Response

Apply It:
Where you have sensed a disconnect between the words you sing at church and the life you live, confess. Take the time at church to examine the words and make a commitment to God that you will mean and live the words you are singing. And when you don't follow through, use the song time to ask Jesus to help you live out these lyrics more than you currently do. A prayer of confession and a humble cry for help is a sweet fragrance of worship to God. He loves brutal honesty. The Israelites were not approaching worship that way—and it stunk. Learn from them and worship in such a way that God is eager to receive it.

Two Questions:
1. What are some aspects of your life (attitudes, actions) that don't match up with the song lyrics you sing at church?
2. What do you need to say to God about that before you sing Him another song?

Week 2 - Days 6-7:
Worship Is Something We Do Together

You have probably heard about or even know a guy who likes to "worship" on the lake fishing, or on the golf course golfing, or on his favorite couch watching, or at the ballfield parenting. I know plenty of these guys and gals who can think of a lot of meaningful and great things to do on Sundays that don't include attending church. The good news is that worship is something we do 24/7 inside or outside and is not confined to the four walls of a church building. In fact, I would agree that some of the moments where I have been most in awe of God and His creativity have been while looking at an ocean or a mountain or a 525-yard dogleg left par 5. We can most definitely connect with God deeply in nature.

But here's the bad news: You're missing out. In fact, it is arrogant to consistently not attend church if you're a follower of Jesus. It's that simple.

The Scripture:
"Let us consider how we may spur one another on toward love and good deeds, not giving up meeting together, as some are in the habit of doing, but encouraging one another—and all the more as you see the Day approaching."— Hebrews 10:24-25, NIV

What It Says About Worship:
Meeting together is important. Worshiping God by encouraging and spurring others on and in turn being encouraged and spurred on by others is commanded.

My Devoted Response

When we choose something else over church, we miss out on the real gift of community. We are saying, in essence, "I can do life alone, thank you very much. I don't need the community of believers. And they don't need me. And if they do, I don't really care. I'm good." Does that sound arrogant? This seems to be what the writer of Hebrews was implying.

King David understood the importance of congregational worship and tried to lead by example on this also. In Psalm 35:18 he wrote, "I will thank you in front of the great assembly. I will praise you before all the people" (NLT). This was the king. The most powerful man in the world letting everybody know that worshiping alone, on a lake, at a game, on a couch, on the fourteenth fairway was not sufficient. He was going to praise God in public, out loud, in a crowd. Why was David so insistent on this? I wonder if it might be that he was making sure everybody around him knew that all the glory for his life, his power, his fame, and his fortune were God's. He was prioritizing public worship in his life.

Apply It:

The writer of Hebrews indicated that some Christians were already in the habit of missing church. That's how it happens, isn't it? We miss once for vacation. We miss again for a sickness. We miss again for a game or an event. We get free tickets to a concert. We have a work function we can't miss. A friend invites us to dinner or a show. We catch one quick weekend out of town on Labor Day. We are exhausted one week and just need a break. Our kid joins a team that travels. Before long, what used to be a church/worship/community habit has been replaced by a new habit: missing out.

You are missing out on receiving encouragement, on growing, on declaring God's goodness in your life, and on helping others. Yes, all those things can happen outside of church. But the author of Hebrews was clear: you need to consistently attend church, you are going to need it more as time goes on, and church is the venue for giving and receiving what God has for your life.

So why not turn this back around? Reprioritize. Cancel the trip. Skip a game. Turn down the tickets. Take the red eye. And choose the path King David and the writer of Hebrews marked out for us. That path leads to church . . . and to a better you . . . and to worship.

Three Questions:
1. Why do you go to church?
2. What do you have that keeps you from attending church more consistently?
3. If you go to church every week, who else can you encourage, or spur on to love and good deeds, while you are together at church this weekend?

Week 3 - Day 1: Through Jesus, For Jesus

"You need to sing more of the great old hymns," advised the sweet, but direct woman who attended my church. She confronted me the Sunday of my controversial decision to start singing a few songs that were not in the hymnal. As a pastor who leads worship songs, one of the things I love most (sarcasm alert) is when people give their detailed suggestions/complaints about the volume in our services, or the song selection, or the instrumentation, or the clothing choices of the people on the platform. It makes it even better when the "suggestions" are made about two minutes before the service starts.

The twenty-year-old version of myself probably didn't handle the moment all that well. With all my youthful energy, I replied, "Why?"

What followed was a list of reasons the old songs were better than the new ones: More theology, rich history, beautiful lyrics. Plus, she just didn't like those new Seven-Eleven songs. You know, the ones where you sing seven words eleven times.

"Ah, now I get it. So, you *prefer* the older songs." I took special care to overemphasize and lengthen my use of the word prefer. She did not appreciate my tone. And looking back, I don't appreciate it either. Reflecting on that moment, it is clear to me now that this charming woman was approaching worship incorrectly. Oh, trust me, I was too. We had the same problem. We were, each in our own way, focused on what we wanted. I wanted the new, because it was new, and I was young. She wanted the old, because she was familiar with it, and it meant something to her. I wanted progress so I could make my mark on the church and the worship experience. She wanted to hold things back and slow things down because with each new song she was, in her mind, losing a part of her heritage. Unfortunately, we both had it wrong. The mission of singing songs in church has never been progress or heritage or making a mark. It is much simpler and deeper than that.

The Scripture:
"Christ is the visible image of the invisible God. He existed before anything was created and is supreme over all creation, for through him God created everything in the heavenly realms and on earth. He made the things we can see and the things we can't see—such as thrones, kingdoms, rulers, and authorities in the unseen world. Everything was created through him and for him."—Colossians 1:15-16, NLT.

What It Says About Worship:
Here is what the woman and I both missed. We assumed the songs of worship were solely for us, as if the lyrics, the tune, and the instrumentation were ours to own and control. But this passage says everything was created through Jesus and for Jesus. That includes worship. God made worship and He made it for Himself. It's not about us. It's not about our preferences or style choices. It's not about what we think it should look, sound, or feel like. There have been plenty of times I have sat in a church service and thought through all the things I would do differently if I were in charge. But then I must remind myself: Everything going on in this room right now was made through Jesus and for Jesus.

My Devoted Response

I'm not the audience. He is. I'm not the focus. He is. I'm not the target of this moment. He is.

This passage also suggests that when we worship something other than God—money, family, sports, work, hobbies, or preferences—we are stealing from the Creator of those things. Worship is for Him. It is His. He is the Creator of it and should be the object of it. Because worship was created for Jesus, He should always get our mind's attention and heart's affection. Our whole lives must be built around His mission for us on this earth. Do most believers you know focus their lives on Christ? Or do you see people build their lives around their child's sport? Or around career advancement? Or around their money or their family? When you and I focus more on, and make more decisions based on, something other than Jesus, we are worshiping that thing instead of Christ. In fact, when we get so focused on our style preferences at church that it takes away our ability to focus on Him, we are worshiping that preference. We must remember that worship is for Jesus and not for anybody or anything else. So, when your mind's attention and heart's affection wander away from Him and on to something else, you have stolen worship away from the One who created it.

Apply It:

Whether we are all alone, in a group, or in a public congregational setting, worship is always intended for Christ. Next time you feel the urge to give in to feeling critical or frustrated over something going on in your church service, first focus on Jesus. Worship Him. Tell Him how great He is and why you have decided to give your life to Him. Thank Him. Use the song lyrics as a springboard to an honest, authentic time of conversation with God. And after you have done all of that, notice your perspective. My guess is that you'll feel a little better about the time you've spent. You will have reminded yourself, as I have had to remind myself, that worship is made through—and for—Jesus.

Three Questions:
1. In what ways have I judged a worship leader or team?
2. What preferences of mine do I need to let go of or loosen?
3. Am I worshiping anything in my life other than Jesus?

Week 3 - Day 2: Satan Wants Worship

I have a really good friend named Thomas. He loves Jesus and has served as a non-paid minister in churches almost his entire life. In his twenties Thomas met the woman of his dreams—Sara. They started dating and got to know each other's families well. As time went on, and they grew more serious, Thomas decided he wanted to marry Sara. One night under the stars, Thomas popped the question, Sara said yes, and they set a wedding date for a little less than a year away.

As engaged people do, they continued to spend more and more time together. Years before, always wanting to please God with every aspect of his life, Thomas had made a vow of sexual purity until marriage. But the closer he and Sara got to being married, the more difficult this vow became. Ultimately, Thomas broke that vow. He set up a time to talk to me about it and he poured out his heart about how he felt so guilty and broken. One of the worst consequences was that he felt like a hypocrite any time he tried to worship God at church. Through ongoing discussions and a lot of prayer, Thomas was able to forgive himself, seek and embrace God's forgiveness, and worship fully again without his failure always being on his mind.

Maybe you have experienced something that made you feel like Thomas felt. Shame from breaking a vow or promise. Maybe you stole something or betrayed someone. Perhaps you gave yourself to something unhealthy. It starts with a temptation, an offer you can't refuse, and the next thing you know, life as you know it no longer exists.

Temptations. Everyone experiences them. Some are stronger than others, but all are meant to do two things: destroy you and steal worship from God. In our weakest moments an offer comes our way. What we do with that offer says a lot about our commitment to God. It says a lot about our worship.

The Scripture:
"The devil led [Jesus] up to a high place and showed him in an instant all the kingdoms of the world. And he said to him, 'I will give you all their authority and splendor; it has been given to me, and I can give it to anyone I want to. If you worship me, it will all be yours'"—Luke 4:5-7, NIV.

What It Says About Worship:
This is one of the most incredibly strange stories in the Bible. After forty days of fasting, Jesus goes with Satan up to a high place and looks over some land. Satan offers him the land and control over it if Jesus will only worship him. Here are the facts in that moment: Jesus is God, He knows He's God, and He knows that all this land and control are His anyway—He made it. He also knows that Satan gets destroyed in the end.

So why would the enemy make such a flimsy offer? It's like me at various times in early 21st century offering Tom Brady, Aaron Rodgers, and Eli Manning a crisp new ten-dollar bill if they'll just retire and quit beating the Cowboys. Did Satan really think Jesus would lay down his whole future for power over a few people? It seems like a long shot.

Here's what the enemy knew in that moment: Jesus was 100

My Devoted Response

percent God, but also 100 percent man. He was challenging the humanity of Jesus, not His deity. If he could just get Jesus, who was already weakened from the forty-day fast, to break, Satan knew Jesus' potential would forever be weakened. God had a master plan for Jesus that included saving the whole world. If there was any way Satan could bring an end to this mission, then in his mind, humanity could forever be separated from God.

God's plan for your life might not include saving humanity from certain eternal demise (unless you're Batman, in which case I would ask you to once and for all defeat all the bad guys because the constantly changing series of movies is getting tiresome). But God's plan for you might not be that far off. When God made you, He made you with a specific set of talents, gifts, and personality to live in a way that influences people for good. He has a mission for your life that is not just about you. It's a hero's life. It's full of adventure and beauty and struggle and victory. God didn't create you to be born, to breathe, to make money, to retire, and then to die. You have something within you that is in no one else. And when you live this life God has mapped out for you, you will arrive at your closing breaths with peace, knowing you really lived . . . and the world will be better because of it.

The enemy, however, is determined to distract you from your life mission by distracting your heart away from God. Satan realizes it's a long shot that you would fully deny Jesus and worship him. But if he can take your eyes off God, then he can derail you from your future. And he's not quite as obvious as he was with Jesus. He doesn't walk up and introduce himself. He just picks away at your weaknesses like He did with Jesus in his hungry state. He taps into your loneliness and shows you a tantalizing relationship that looks and feels right on the surface, but it is not. Your greed gets challenged when an opportunity to make a lot of money presents itself, but it might not be totally above board. In your insecurity and heartbroken state, a substance that helps you feel good is within reach, but it slowly alters your mind. In essence, you are standing on a mountain with the enemy, and he is offering you the land, control of your own life, your own body, and your own mind. If you answer yes, the payoff is immediate and awesome.

The effect, however, is a dismantling of the future God has in store for you—a journey into a future where your best life is revealed.

In this story Jesus is showing us what the essence of worship really is. It is saying no to the temporary and yes to the eternal. It is constantly reminding the enemy that you are on a journey that will outlive him. The enemy desires your worship, just as he desired Christ's. And though you may not be breaking out the Ouija board anytime soon and offering cat sacrifices to the enemy, he still wants to subtly distract you from your future that God has already mapped out for you.

So, in those moments of temptation when your future is hanging in the balance, do what Jesus did. Say, "No! I will not worship you by accepting something so temporary and small when I have an incredible journey of faith ahead of me." In saying no to that temptation, you are saying yes to worshiping Jesus.

Apply It:
Today as you pray and interact in life, and this weekend, when you stand in church and sing songs and hear a message, remember Satan is waging a battle for your very soul. Commit yourself again to God's plan for your life. Remem-

ber, His path is the adventurous one that is leading you toward a full and abundant life.

Three Questions:
1. What heroic future for your life has God spoken to you about? If you don't know, what heroic future do you sometimes dream about?
2. What temptation does the enemy most often place before you?
3. How will you worship next time you face this temptation? In other words, the next time this temptation arrives, and it will, what Scripture can you quote to give you strength against the enemy? What action steps can you decide on now that will help you say no to the temptation and yes to God?

Week 3 - Day 3: Worship and Fear

What are you afraid of?

Some people are afraid of the color yellow. It's called xanthophobia. Others freak out at their own navels—omphalophobia. Maybe you know someone with coulrophobia, the fear of clowns. I have nomophobia. It's the tragic fear of not having cell coverage. A dark road in the middle of nowhere with the words No Service laughing at me from the top left corner of my iPhone screen strikes terror in my heart. Just thinking about it is causing me to have chills right now.

Maybe for you it's spiders or heights, public speaking, or elevators. When I was a kid, I had a fear of my dad's belt. I was well aware of its power and how it felt as it struck my backside. I also knew how to arouse its fury—it wasn't really all that difficult. One time, during a prayer before a meal, I got up, walked across the room, grabbed a toy truck that I was supposed to wait to play with until after we'd eaten, and got back to my seat just before my dad said, "Amen." I was feeling pretty good and accomplished for about ten seconds. That was when my inner fool showed itself and caused me to hold the truck over my head, revealing to the whole family how I had so deftly made my way across the room and back during such a short prayer. My beltophobia was then awakened to an extremely high level as my dad took me into another room and reminded me that prayer time was for prayers and truck time was for never again.

It seems like in all our fears, we possess a built-in level of respect for the things of which we are afraid. If you're afraid of spiders, it's because you respect their bite and venom. If you fear public speaking, it's because you respect the power of the audience in making you feel nervous or stupid. If you fear your belly button, you're just weird.

An innate fear of something is actually good for us in many instances. I should have had a stronger dose of fear for my go-cart as a kid. I ran it into trees a lot. I flipped it and broke my hand in three places. Another time, while messing with the engine, I cranked it to overdrive while holding on to the back of the thing. I flew fifteen feet through the air before landing on the asphalt parking lot. The fact that I'm alive and lucid these days is a miracle. I finally gained respect—fear—for the go-cart and its ability to make me feel pain.

The Scripture:
"The fear of the Lord is the beginning of wisdom [and] . . . understanding."—Psalm 111:10, NIV
"We ask God to give you complete knowledge of his will and to give you spiritual wisdom and understanding. Then the way you live will always honor and please the Lord, and your lives will produce every kind of good fruit."—Colossians 1:9-10, NLT, emphasis added

What It Says About Worship:
Do you see the progression? Fear leads to wisdom and understanding. Wisdom and understanding lead to living a life that always honors and pleases God. That's a pretty solid definition of worship, by the way. In its most basic sense, fear ultimately leads to worship. First, it leads to wisdom and understanding. Not the earthly, simple form of wisdom or understanding where we get better grades, rise faster in

the corporation, or know lots of facts.

No, fear leads to the kind of wisdom and understanding that only God can give. It's when you see something in life or in Scripture that you would have no way of understanding except God gives you insight or direction. We see Solomon with that kind of wisdom when he almost sawed a baby in half (see 1 Kings 3:16-28). If you don't know what I'm talking about, take a minute and read that crazy story. Seriously, it's brilliant and full of wisdom only God can give.

Then, as Colossians 1:9-10 tells us, when we receive wisdom and understanding from God, our lives start to worship Him naturally. It's not as though we must try hard or work up a worship fever with a good set from the latest and greatest church worship band. We just start living in ways that honor and please the Lord. It's beautiful. It's simple. And it starts with fear.

Apply It:
A few years ago, I started praying for wisdom every day. Try it. Start your day with this prayer: "God, give me wisdom today." Jesus' brother James wrote in chapter 1, verse 5 of his letter that if we ask for wisdom, we will receive it from God. Cool! So then, ask for wisdom and understanding. Then watch…as you start to receive it, your life will naturally begin to worship God.

And another thing: fear the Lord. How do you develop fear? Fear occurs naturally when you have a better understanding of the power of something or someone. Try reading Genesis 1 and 2 on occasion, or Revelation. The Bible starts and finishes with strong demonstrations of God's power.

My Devoted Response

It might take a little time, but ultimately you will build up a healthy fear for God, based on your respect of Him. Then as you ask for it, wisdom and understanding will grow. And ultimately your life, all of it, will always honor and please God. When that happens, your worship offering is going to be better than you ever imagined.

Three Questions:

1. What are three things about God that you honor and respect?
2. In your understanding of the Bible, what story or act of God best demonstrates His power?
3. In what areas of your life do you need God's wisdom the most?

Week 3 - Day 4: Worship Through Thanksgiving and Awe

One of the things my team and I did together for 14 years was to produce the worship experiences for a youth camp in California. Typically, we would have 1,000 to 1,200 people from thirty to thirty-five different churches, many of whom consider this one of their most significant annual experiences with Jesus. My team was tasked with planning the services, writing, casting and directing sketches, writing and editing videos, tying all of the various speaking and musical pieces together, and then orchestrating all of the technology to make it happen.

These days at camp were very long. Our first meeting began at 6:30 a.m. and the days didn't finish until well after 11:00 p.m. each night. Many of the services have run together in my mind as we have produced more than one hundred of them through the years. But one-night stands out more than the others.

The topic of the night was love and how in today's culture we sometimes don't understand what love is. We wrote a thirteen-minute sketch modeled after the movie The Breakfast Club. The students in detention had to discuss love and then each write a paper on what love meant to them. Each character had a personal story that led to their fractured, but emotional answer to the question, "What is love?"

My Devoted Response

The students nailed the sketch! All of them were from my church so I was additionally proud. This scene was placed in the middle of the pastor's message, about 80 percent into it. So, just a few minutes after it was over, he asked the student congregation to consider how they might respond to the perfect love of God. Would they be willing to trust Jesus' love and give their lives to Him?

The pastor gave the invitation to the students: "Will you stand where you are, come to the front of the stage, and ask Jesus to give you a new life?" With my headphones on, communicating to the tech team from the back of the meeting space, I had a good vantage point to see who might stand and walk to the front of the room to pray and begin a relationship with Christ. Before he could even finish the question, two girls near the front and to my left, stood and started walking forward. It was dark in the room, but within a few seconds I thought I knew who they were. I got on the headphones to ask Cami, who was the stage manager and had a front-row seat. She confirmed it. After having just spent thirteen minutes discussing love in front of the whole room, two of the girls who had performed the sketch were now walking forward to receive the love from God that was being offered to them!

None of us had considered the fact that two of our actors weren't yet believers. But we were excited! When the service was over, our team all ran up to hug them and welcome them into the Kingdom of God. There was a lot of crying and celebrating and awe of what God had done.

That night after we had our closing meetings, I was with a few of our team members, and we were walking back to the apartments. We talked about the evening and how those girls had spoken on love in the sketch without really knowing much about God's love. Usually at the end of one of those nights we would all be completely exhausted, but that night was different.

We were being buoyed by a feeling that was stronger than tiredness; it was thankfulness. We were genuinely thankful and in awe for all God had done, and that He was so kind as to let us play a small part in this magnificent day.

The Scripture:
"Since we are receiving a Kingdom that is unshakable, let us be thankful and please God by worshiping him with holy fear and awe."—Hebrews 12:28, NLT

What It Says About Worship:
Leading up to this passage in Hebrews, the author had been writing about the amazing inheritance we have because of Christ's blood. He remembered back to Mt. Sinai where Moses received God's commands. God's voice shook the earth in those days. The author then shared how so many things in our lives, the created things on earth, are going to be shaken again, and the only thing that will remain is the Kingdom of God. In response, this Hebrews passage gives us two ways to respond in worship to this amazing reality of God's eternal Kingdom: be thankful and live with respect and awe of God.

Are you a thankful person? Is it easy for you to see the blessings in your life? You may be one who has lived through many difficult times. When we suffer through relational, financial, and physical problems, it is often difficult to see anything good. Here is what the author of Hebrews was trying to communicate, and I echo to you: nothing on this earth can shake your ultimate future. If you are a follower of Jesus, you will receive from Him an eternity in heaven.

My Devoted Response

Not only that, but you are also living in His Kingdom today. And you're a child of the King, which means you have all the rights of a prince or princess. While others live aimlessly, hoping for a few good days or years with no real idea of the future, you have a different story! You are a permanent resident of a Kingdom! No political party, leadership structure, financial struggle, mean person, or demonic power can shake that. Does that make you thankful? A grateful heart is worship to God. Your moments of awe and wonder over the reality of your present and future are worship to Him.

Apply It:

Close your eyes and thank God. Like that night at camp, after the amazing evening of worship and evangelism, our team took time to be thankful. This is a discipline we must repeat over and over to the point of mastery. Thank Him for everything you can think of. Don't ask Him to solve the world's problems or even your own. Just be thankful. As you begin to tell God about all the amazing things He has done in and for you, let your irritations and frustrations be replaced with a true spirit of thanksgiving. That gratitude will lead to a true respect and awe for God and His ways. Also, the next time you are at church, start with this discipline of being thankful. It's the proper way to enter the house of God. In Psalm 100:4, the psalmist instructed us to "enter his gates with thanksgiving and his courts with praise" (NIV, emphasis added).

The way of thanksgiving and awe is not always easy. It takes work. The darkness of life can cloud the way of awe. Don't let that happen to you. Choose to be thankful. Take the time to be in awe. This is worship.

Three Questions:
1. List ten things for which you are thankful today. In what ways do those things bring you gratitude?
2. What are some things that sometimes get in the way of you being thankful?
3. Why do you think being in awe of God is important?

Week 3 - Day 5:
Worship Should Never Be Rules-Based

When my daughter, Finley, was almost finished with fifth grade, I asked her what she was most excited about in terms of finishing elementary school and heading into middle school. She didn't even have to think about it. She said, "No more walking in lines!"

By the time kids get to fifth grade, they have had just about all the line walking they can handle. It's time to express their freedom and rid themselves of that childish kindergarten rule.

Life is like that, isn't it? When we are young, we have tons of rules we have to follow.

Don't unplug things.

Don't cross the street without holding Mom's hand.

Sit down at the table when you eat.

Thankfully, as we get older those rules go away. But then they are replaced by older kid rules:

Be home by eleven.

Don't drive with your friends in your car.

In every stage of life, we have rules, until finally, after almost two decades of will-crippling boundaries, we move away from home and find freedom. At last! No. More Rules. Do you remember that day?

Over time, however, we decide that some rules were good ones: Treat people with respect, cover your mouth when you cough, and wash your hands before you eat. But other rules were only there for a season. Can you imagine seeing a thirty-four-year-old man choosing not to cross any streets because his mom's hand isn't there to hold? How about a twenty-year-old woman who refuses to unplug and move the lamps around her apartment for fear of deadly shock? Neither of these scenarios makes sense. And yet sometimes we view the form of church services like that: we see them as rules to be obeyed for all time and in every culture.

The Scripture:
"The Lord says, 'These people . . . honor me with their lips, but their hearts are far from me. Their worship of me is based on merely human rules they have been taught.'"— Isaiah 29:13, NIV

What It Says About Worship:
As was typical, the Israelites were worshiping other gods, not believing the one and only true God could save them. So, they basically decided to go through the motions as God's chosen people. They were still doing churchy things, but at the end of the day, it didn't mean much to them. Their parents had taught them how to go to God's house, pray the prayers, sing the songs, and give the gifts. They followed the "rules," but all of it was based on tradition, not on the true and humble attitude of their hearts.

The Bible contains a lot of good rules for us to follow—but nowhere does it prescribe which songs we are supposed to sing. Or how many singers should be on stage. Or what size our video screens should be. Or much of anything else when it comes to the functionality of our public expressions of worship. In fact, we don't have one complete church service anywhere in the Bible that gives us direction on how the early followers worshiped.

But we do have a lot of Scripture that focuses on the heart and how we are to show up to worship. If you're still struggling over singing too many or not enough hymns or modern songs, it's probably time to let that go. The hymns or modern songs you love are awesome, but they are merely human rules taught by man. Your favorite instrument (be it drums, organ, electric guitar, or saxophone) is awesome, but it's merely a human rule taught by man. Whether you love the repeatable form of liturgy or a more free-flowing style, that's awesome too. But neither one of those was dictated to us in God's Word. God is a lot less concerned with which songs you sing, the order in which you sing them, how many people sing them from the platform, or how you perform them stylistically than He is with the full devotion of your heart.

Apply It:
If you are getting hung up on some of these human rules, let them go. Worship is not about that. Stop honoring God with only your lips. When we require a form that is pleasing to us that we have been taught by someone, that's what we are doing. Please try not to be distracted by the form, and instead focus on your own heart. If you have the freedom to do this, over the next few months, pick four different churches to attend that have very different worship "styles" and commit to worshiping fully in each of those settings. Then return to your own church fully ready and thankful to give God, and the congregation, your all. Remember that the form and the songs can be different. God receives every

style and form because He honors the heart of the worshiper more than our man-made rules.

Three Questions:

1. What are some aspects of your church services that you love?
2. What parts of your services would you like to change or delete? Why? Are there any things you would like to add?
3. Of the things you love in church, or would like to see, which are mandated in the Bible, and which are humans' efforts to honor God, but not explicitly biblical?

My Devoted Response

Week 3 – Days 6-7: Chosen to Worship

"You're suiting up with varsity tomorrow night."

"I'm what?"

"We need you to be on varsity tomorrow night. Be ready to play."

"Yes, coach."

That was the extent of my conversation with the varsity football coach about 5 minutes after the last JV game I would ever play. What transpired over the next few weeks was completely unexpected. 23 hours after that short exchange, as we came out of the locker room after halftime, I was and would remain the starting quarterback for our high school team. Those two comments from the coach kind of changed my life.

Looking back at it now it wasn't a huge thing in the scope of life. Eventually most JV players end up on varsity if they play long enough. It was more the way it happened in the middle of the season when the varsity team was really struggling. And the phrase, "we need you on varsity tomorrow night" did not mean that he was one player short of the required minimum. It assumed something much more profound. He needed a spark. He needed something different than what he currently had. In essence, he needed to win. What he was saying was that it wasn't enough for me to wear a jersey…he had plenty of people doing that. It wasn't enough for me to play the position of quarterback… he already had three people who knew the plays. What he needed, and I knew it very well without him saying it, was for me to perform, and perform a lot better than the other guy. The team was winless at the time, 0-4.

By the end of the season we had almost swept the table, climbed into second place in our district, beaten our biggest rivals who were ranked #8 in Texas and squeezed our way into the playoffs. All because of me? Of course not. Anybody who knows anything about football, or any other team sport knows that everyone must perform well to win… not just the leader. I'm certain that if the other guy would have stayed in at quarterback, the team would have improved and fared very well. Everybody raised their game as the season progressed. So here is the principle of this little 135-pound sophomore getting called up to play with the big boys: If we had kept losing, I would have been back on JV. Why? Because I was called up to play hard. To leave it all on the field. To be better than the opponent. To win.

The Scripture:
"But you are a chosen people, a royal priesthood, a holy nation, God's special possession THAT YOU MAY declare the praises of Him who called you out of darkness and into His marvelous light." —I Peter 2:9, NIV, emphasis added

What the Bible Says About Worship:
You have been given much. A seat at the table of God. Forgiveness by the blood of Jesus. Counsel offered by the Holy Spirit. Wisdom when you ask for it. You are the object of God's affection. Peter says it clearly here: You are chosen, royal, holy, and possessed by God. But just like me being chosen and called out to be a varsity quarterback, you were also given a responsibility. Something is expected of you.

My Devoted Response

You need to perform. You weren't just called out to wear the Christian jersey or increase the number of Christians on the planet. You were chosen, made holy, and possessed by God SO THAT you could declare His praises.

He called you out of darkness and into His marvelous light. There is really only one response to that: worship! The verse in I Peter calls it, "declaring His praises." You were given a jersey, a name on the jersey and a chance to start on the greatest team ever assembled. Will you treat this gift with laziness, only to work fairly hard on it at church most Sundays? Or will you take this golden opportunity to work the hardest, pray the hardest, and worship God with all you've got every single day?

Apply it:
Are you having a good day? Declare the praises of God to the people around you. Are you healthy? Give honor to God for that. Is your life better because of His life in you? Make sure you don't keep quiet about God's goodness. You were called and set apart as a possession of God. That's amazing news! But He's not just chosen you to be on the team. He has actually given you a really important role – to speak of His goodness to everyone and worship Him as you do.

Before you finish, read this meaningful take on I Peter 2:9 by Eugene Peterson in The Message:
"But you are the ones chosen by God, chosen for the high calling of priestly work, chosen to be a holy people, God's instruments to do his work and speak out for him, to tell others of the night-and-day difference he made for you—from nothing to something, from rejected to accepted."

Three Questions:

1. In what ways are you declaring the praises of God to the people around you?
2. Who has God placed around you that needs to hear how good God is?
3. What are two or three ways you can declare God's praises to the people around you this week?

My Devoted Response

Week 4 - Day 1: Worship Requires Unity

When I was much younger in my worship leading experience, I used to wave my arms up, down, left, and right to keep the piano player and the congregation all in perfect time. If I didn't wave my arms in that fashion, the congregation wouldn't understand when to put the words to the notes and the piano player would go completely off the rails. It never occurred to me that people sing along to songs on the radio all the time, or even acapella while standing in the shower. And in none of those instances do they follow a person giving the obligatory up, down, left, and right arm motions.

One Sunday as I was waving away, I got to the end of the last song, and it was time for the message. Since the pastor and I had not discussed the service earlier in the week, I looked over to his seating area to give him the nod. For you non-worship leaders or pastors, this is a worldwide standard signal for "I did my part. It's your turn now." However, when I looked, there was no pastor. I panicked a little. Nearing the final line of the final verse, I looked frantically around the room to see if he'd switched things up and moved elsewhere. A quick but casual look around revealed that he was not anywhere and that I was in trouble. I had no other songs ready to go.

Thinking fast, I did the only "spiritual" thing I could think of, and said I felt led we should sing that last verse again, only this time more slowly and meaningfully. I was proud of myself to come up with the vamp, especially the slower part so it would give the pastor more time to come back from the bathroom or wherever he was.

Thirty seconds later we were nearing the end again and still no pastor. Now I felt less stressed and more frustrated. Where is he, I wondered as I rescanned the room. I found him in the back, kneeling behind the crowd. It was clear he wasn't coming up front any time soon. I had to vamp again. "Now just the ladies sing the verse again." Finally, when we had sung some variation of the final verse four times and people were starting to assume I had lost it, my pastor walked up to the front and began to preach. After the service I questioned him as to what he had been doing.

"My wife and I got into a bit of a fight this morning before I left for church and I said a thing or two I shouldn't have said," he admitted. "I realized that before I worshiped God by preaching, I needed to go and apologize and ask for her forgiveness."

What an amazing moment. I had a leader who was that open to his own weaknesses and so biblical in the way he handled them. I thanked him for being a good example and showing me, a new minister, how to work through hard times. Then I looked him in the eye and said, "Don't ever do that again. Next time, get your stuff together before you come to church! I don't have extra songs hanging out in my back pocket."

The Scripture:
"If you are offering your gift at the altar and there remember that your brother or sister has something against you, leave your gift there in front of the altar.

First go and be reconciled to them; then come and offer your gift."—Matthew 5:23-24, NIV

What It Says About Worship:
Unity is required for worship. Jesus is clear in these verses. He is not interested in accepting our offering (singing, giving, preaching, teaching, etc.) unless we have our relationships in good shape. He's not just speaking hyperbolically here.

Jesus literally means that unity needs to be in place before we offer God anything. My pastor understood that principle. He had three options: (1) preach anyway, deciding he could fix the relationship with his wife later in the afternoon; (2) run to his car and hide; (3) do what he did—leave his gift in front of the altar, reconcile things with his wife, and then return to offer the gift. Which path produced the worship that God was willing to receive? No question: it was path #3.

In Romans 15:5-6, NIV, Paul wrote, "May the God who gives endurance and encouragement give you the same attitude of mind toward each other as Christ Jesus had, SO THAT with one mind and one voice you may glorify the God and Father of our Lord Jesus Christ (emphasis added).

This passage informs us of the prerequisite to worship that unity really is. As a kid, you wash your hands so that mom will let you eat. As a teenager you pass your driving test so you can legally drive and be awesome. These are prerequisites. In college, you can't take Spanish 3 until you have passed Spanish 2. You can't take Calculus 2 until you've passed Calculus 1. And in life, you can't worship God unless you have the same attitude toward the other believers around you that Jesus has for us.

Apply It:
Fight for peace. If you have a dangling relationship, restore it. If you have said or done something wrong, confess it. If you have a cold war going on with a coworker or friend, go make peace. It's not just between you and that person. Worship is on the line. If you've been attempting to worship God with a broken relationship in your life, you more than likely have experienced some obstacles in your connection to Christ. But if you will forgive, confess, and restore unity, God will start to accept what you offer Him, and worship will finally be unleashed.

Two Questions:
1. What relationship needs to be restored so you can bring God an offering of worship He will accept?
2. What steps do you need to take to restore unity?

My Devoted Response

Week 4 - Day 2: Worship Leads to Repentance and Mission

Think back to the most powerful worship service you have ever experienced.

Where was it? Who was leading from the platform? Who were you with that day? Can you remember what songs you sang or what message you heard? What did you experience that causes you to say it was powerful? Was the music especially good? Were the lights just right? Did the lead singer or preacher say the right words at just the right time? Maybe you don't remember any of those details, but you do remember the presence of God and how strangely impactful He was that day.

I love services like this where I leave having experienced a lump in my throat, a deep connection to God's Spirit, and a feeling of hope. It reminds me that my heart still beats for God. As I leave after days like that, I am somehow more committed to God's plan for my life. Have you had moments like that at church?

There is a gathering like this in the Bible. It's not an official Sunday morning kind of church service, but it is definitely an experience to be remembered. Some crazy things are recorded in this story that are so profound, that the man who watched it happen turned his life around and became fully committed to God.

The Scripture:

"It was in the year King Uzziah died that I saw the Lord. He was sitting on a lofty throne, and the train of his robe filled the Temple. Attending him were mighty seraphim, each having six wings. With two wings they covered their faces, with two they covered their feet, and with two they flew. They were calling out to each other, 'Holy, holy, holy is the Lord of Heaven's Armies! The whole earth is filled with his glory!' Their voices shook the Temple to its foundations, and the entire building was filled with smoke.

"Then I said, 'It's all over! I am doomed, for I am a sinful man. I have filthy lips, and I live among a people with filthy lips. Yet I have seen the King, the Lord of Heaven's Armies.'

"Then one of the seraphim flew to me with a burning coal he had taken from the altar with a pair of tongs. He touched my lips with it and said, 'See, this coal has touched your lips. Now your guilt is removed, and your sins are forgiven.' Then I heard the Lord asking, 'Whom should I send as a messenger to this people? Who will go for us?'

"I said, 'Here I am. Send me.'"—Isaiah 6:1-8, NLT

What It Says About Worship:

We could discuss that God is on a throne, which means He oversees everything. We could talk about the worship chants of the seraphim. We could investigate the guilt removing that takes place in God's presence, or even His robe and what that signifies. But let's focus on Isaiah's only two verbal responses to all he saw. Can you imagine being Isaiah in this moment? He was just chillin', when suddenly, he saw the Lord! That's crazy enough, but it wasn't over. The Scripture mentions a big robe, strange angelic beings, a repetitive worship chant, the shaking of the earth, and smoke filling the space where they were. Isaiah had never been to a worship experience like this before. Nobody had!

My Devoted Response

This was when Isaiah finally conjured up some words. I think he blurted them out. "It's all over. I am doomed. I am a sinful man. I have filthy lips and I live among a people with filthy lips." Isaiah experienced holiness and it ruined him. When we encounter holiness, we realize how unholy we really are. Darkness is unmasked when the light enters. Isaiah could have said to God, "Look how great You are! I worship You! You are mighty!" But that wasn't his response. It was brokenness, sadness over his own depravity. I wonder if you have felt this way in God's presence; you had a crystal-clear picture of your own absolute lostness. I have. I hope you will experience this feeling if you haven't. Isaiah needed in this moment to be humiliated so he could get to his next statement.

But first, one of the seraphim seared Isaiah's lips with a hot coal, forgiving his sin. You see, when we stop trying to justify our goodness and we simply confess our sin, feeling true brokenness over it, God comes to our rescue and forgives, heals, and restores us. First comes our honesty. Then comes God's healing.

The Lord asked a question next. "Who shall I send as a messenger to this people? Who will go for us?" Isaiah knew the question was directed to him. I imagine after all he had experienced, he was eager to answer, "Here I am. Send me!"

Five words. That's all it took for Isaiah to fully surrender himself to God's purposes for his life. This is what the passage says about worship: the holiness of God leads us to repentance and the forgiveness of God leads us on His mission. Remember it was in this atmosphere of the purest worship that all of this happened. There were seraphim and chanting and sincere awe—so much so that smoke appeared, and things shook. And as Isaiah watched, he worshiped, and it led him to repentance and mission.

Apply It:
Repent. You're not perfect. Nobody is. And then say yes to God. Isaiah didn't receive a clear roadmap from the Lord at that moment. He just heard a question, "Who will go?" God might not be giving you a clear roadmap either. That's okay. His plan for your life is the best plan for your life. You don't need to know what next week, next month, or the next decade looks like. Right now, and again tomorrow, the next day, and the day after that, respond to God's holiness by repenting of your sin and then respond to His forgiveness by saying, "Yes, Lord. No matter what You ask, I will do it."

Three Questions:
1. Do you remember a time when you recognized your sin in a profound way? Think about that time and reflect on what led up to that clarity.
2. Toward what mission might God be leading you?
3. Are you prepared to say yes to God today, no matter what His ask might be?

Week 4 - Day 3: Worship and Temples

At some point, every Christian should have the "privilege" of serving on their church's building committee. Maybe you have had that opportunity and you know why privilege might not be the perfect word to explain it. Oh, it's entertaining! In a conversation with a building committee member years ago, I remember her wondering aloud, "How is it that I, a non-builder, non-accountant, non-creative person has been asked to help build something very architecturally complex, financially challenging, and aesthetically beautiful? What could go wrong?" We had a good laugh about that—and about the unique challenges any team faces because of the varying personalities of its members.

I have served on two such teams. I was the team leader on one and the "staff liaison" on the other. One team lasted two years. The other lasted nine. Of course, we faced challenges like design disagreements, cost overruns, conflicting priorities, and weather delays, to name a few. But one of the most difficult issues to navigate in each of my building experiences was this: How much is too much?

Typically, most team members come to the table with a total dollar amount in mind, a style they like, and another church building they want to emulate. Also, they bring strong opinions about how opulent or stripped down a church building should be. Some would say that a building is a necessary evil that takes money away from the real mission, so spending as little as possible is the best way forward. Some might say, "If it wasn't for the fact that it sometimes rains on Sundays, it would be more prudent for us to meet outdoors. After all, Jesus Himself had no place to lay His head (Luke 9:58), so let's not go overboard in our spending." And then others fall at the other end of the continuum: "Let's build an amazing edifice to our God who created all things. The best materials, the most beautiful artwork, and the top-of-the-line sound and lighting systems." You might hear this person say, "After all, in today's dollars, Solomon's Temple held more than $200 billion in silver and gold alone (1 Chronicles 22, 29). We should spare no expense on building a facility to honor His name."

You, more than likely, live somewhere between these two extremes, and with a degree of pragmatism that is all your own. Everyone has an opinion about how much to invest on a building. For instance, I have heard through the years that when you build a worship center, you should spend 10 percent of your overall construction cost on sound, video, and lighting. But that is just someone's opinion based on where they fall on the continuum. My guess is "that guy" sells sound systems.

So how much is too much?

The answer is . . . I don't know. Here's what I do know. After constructing an amazing temple to God, exactly to God's specifications, and spending more than $200 billion to do it, Solomon said this in His prayer of dedication: "Will God really dwell on earth? The heavens, even the highest heaven, cannot contain you. How much less this temple I have built!" (1 Kings 8:27, NIV). After all of Solomon's careful work on the temple and the many thousands of people who helped construct it, he knew that God was bigger than this one facility.

Could it be that we are asking the wrong question? I assume you know that God is not contained to your church building. It is not the location of His Spirit. In Solomon's day it was different. Solomon was investing in the dwelling place of God. I could imagine if God came to me and asked me to build Him a house where He would live, I would try to build a really nice one. But God doesn't "live" in our church buildings.

The Scripture:
"Do you not know that your bodies are temples of the Holy Spirit, who is in you, whom you have received from God? You are not your own; you were bought at a price. Therefore, honor God with your bodies."—1 Corinthians 6:19-20, NIV

What It Says About Worship:
The dwelling place of God, where He is to be honored and worshiped is important. In Solomon's day it was the Holy of Holies inside the Temple. Today, that dwelling place is inside me and inside you. In church life we spend a lot of time talking about the "temples" where we meet on Sundays. We invest in them, show them off, care for them, and keep them as updated as we can afford. Can you say the same for your own temple? Your body is a temple. How are you treating it? In this 1Corinthians passage, Paul spelled out a clear principle: Take care of your body. Keep it away from sin, especially sexual sin. How you treat your body is worship to God. I know I'm meddling here, but I wonder how you would grade yourself on investing and taking care of the temple of the Holy Spirit, which is your body. Churches have dozens of meetings to make sure their temple looks just right, feels just right, and work just right.

Do you put that much thought and investment into your temple?

Apply It:
Offer God this prayer: "God, I know I am not my own. You bought me with Your own blood. I want to honor You with my body. Forgive me where I have treated my body like it was my own." Once you are ready, have a building committee meeting with yourself. Are you doing what you can to have your temple look right? Does it feel right? Is it working right? Are there any unconfessed sins you need to declare? Do you need to clean an area of your temple that's been gathering dust or been neglected all together? Do you need to make some compromises with your time, money, or preferences so you can invest more heavily in this area for a while?

God is interested in the condition of the dwelling place of His Holy Spirit, which is your body. When you honor it, you honor Him. So honestly assess your body. Make a plan. Start getting it to look, feel, and work better. If that includes going to the doctor, God will receive it as worship. If a treadmill is in your future, remember that your sweat is an offering to God. When you eat kale or other green things, God will notice your sacrifice. And if this plan includes freeing yourself from an addiction to an inappropriate physical relationship, let this be your motivation. Every step you take toward a healthier, more yielded temple is an offering of worship to God that He will not only enjoy, but will turn back to you as a blessing.

My Devoted Response

Three Questions:

1. Have you ever thought about the things you do to and with your body as worship?
2. What commitments do you need to make to worship God by honoring Him with your body?
3. What are the small steps of worship you will need to take to achieve the big change you are seeking?

Week 4 - Day 4: Worship Should Often Be Loud

Priests don't like it when their air conditioning vents shake! I was a singer for a wedding in a Catholic church. It was this amazing, beautiful building with high concrete walls, stained glass, ornate pillars, and a giant pipe organ. The song the bride and groom wanted me to sing had an instrumental track, but because the church didn't have a sound system, I had to bring a small portable one.

Three hours before the ceremony, I was getting everything all set and prepared. The priest showed up, walked to me, and asked what I was doing. I told him about the track and singing with a microphone and asked him where I might plug in the mixer. He seemed irritated that I would defile his building with an extension cord, but he reluctantly showed me the plug.

For the sound check, I started the track, adjusting the level to make sure it would sound good in the room. The priest, who was now talking to the florist, swung his head around, and started yelling from the tenth row, "It's too loud!" I stopped the track, apologized, turned it down some, and started it again.

"It's too loud!"

This went on two or three more times until I had to hear it for myself. Maybe there was some sound vortex where all the volume in the room landed on row ten. Leaving the

My Devoted Response

music playing I walked toward the priest. He motioned for me to come to the side wall of the church. "It's too loud!" he said again as he pointed up to an air conditioning vent about fifteen feet above us. The music from the track was causing the vent to vibrate. I explained that I couldn't turn the track down much quieter or nobody would be able to hear it.

Clearly unsatisfied, he headed to the sound mixer to turn it down to a level at which only the first two rows might be able to hear the music if they listened carefully. I decided just to wait until the service started, turn it up, and hope for the best.

When the organ player arrived, who looked to be every bit in her mid-eighties, she and the priest greeted each other warmly, then she headed to the pipe organ. As she played, those pipes made some of the most beautiful and powerful notes I had ever heard. Even the priest was grinning ear to ear. I was spellbound by how much it sounded like Phantom of the Opera in the room.

Except there was a faint, but profound sound I was hearing, a sound that didn't fit in the organ's palette. I walked toward the back of the room and then to the side where I looked up. The organ sounds were shaking the air conditioning vents so strongly you could see them vibrate. I laughed. He didn't mind volume. He minded *my* volume.

The Scripture:
"Praise him with trumpet sound; praise him with lute and harp! Praise him with tambourine and dance; praise him with strings and pipe! Praise him with sounding cymbals; praise him with loud clashing cymbals!

Let everything that has breath praise the Lord! Praise the Lord!"—Psalm 150:3-6, ESV, emphasis added

What It Says About Worship:
Worship should sometimes be offered loudly. No holding back. Not whispering but bellowing the glory of God! We shout at football games. We cheer for someone who sings a great song or performs a beautiful dance. We make loud toasts at weddings and other celebrations. But for some reason, many people feel like church is a place of quiet or reverence. But this Scripture offers a different take on reverence…sometimes it is irreverent to be quiet. If someone is in a church service and leading us to sing about how great God is or about His mercy or the life we have because of His resurrection, we should shout or at least sing it loudly. You can't whisper, "He Is Risen!" or say, "I was blind but now I see," quietly to your neighbor. We were brought from death to life. That is not a message we murmur. In 1 Chronicles 15:16, David "commanded the chiefs of the Levites to appoint their brothers as the singers who should play loudly on musical instruments, on harps and lyres and cymbals, to raise sounds of joy." (ESV) If you don't like drums in the church, or loud electric guitars, or loud pipe organs, you might want to get okay with it. David did not suggest that you worship loudly. He commanded that you do so.

Apply It:
Next time you are in church, sing loudly. Embarrassingly so. Don't hold back. Psalm 98:4 tells us to shout to the Lord! It does not say, "Whisper to the Lord." Don't be afraid. If you sing louder, the people around you might join in, and before you know it your church's worship will be more biblical than ever. And if the volume of the church service is loud, remember that even the volume honors God—at least that's

what the Bible says. In fact, next time you are in church, walk up to the sound man, and congratulate him on turning it up. Let him know he is worshiping God in a biblical way when he cranks it.

Imagine the look on Jesus' face when the band is playing loudly, the singers are singing loudly, and you are joining in at the top of your lungs. Depending on how you sing, it might not sound awesome to a discerning ear, but one thing is for sure, it will sound amazing to God!

Three Questions:
1. What good thing in your life has ever caused you to yell loudly? Think game winning touchdown or child graduating from High School.
2. What aspects of God and His intervention in your life might be as good as whatever you answered on question #1?
3. What is holding you back from worshiping God loudly at church?

Week 4 - Day 5:
God Doesn't Need Your Worship

I'm needy. There, I said it. I'm a needy man. I need water. I need shelter. I need french fries. Not only that, I need people in my life. I need my wife. I need my daughter. I need my friends and coworkers. I need things that make life work better, like a cell phone and a computer. I need sleep. I need a coat when it's cold outside. I need accountability. I need a car to get me where I'm going. I need a GPS to tell me where I'm going. I need a calendar to remind me where I'm going. I need a lot of things. Every single day I'm like one of those baby birds with his little beak open and waiting for his mom or dad to drop a chewed-up worm inside.

I am guessing you need things too. Not only physical things. You need untouchable things, like affirmation, love, and compassion. You need someone to approve of you and show you appreciation. You are incredibly needy because every human is needy. We come out of the womb that way and we live every day from that day until our last in need of something or someone. Somehow, we inherently know that about one another. So, if you are caring, you spend time and energy thinking about ways to affirm others, provide for them, and show them love. You fill their need while they fill yours.

We basically spend our whole lives either pouring into others or being poured into by others. We are like drinking glasses with a certain amount of water in us—always pouring some out and hopefully always receiving some in return.

My Devoted Response

This is natural and normal, and the way God made you and me.

Maybe you have never thought of your life in these terms and haven't realized that you make many decisions based on this reality every day. Sometimes, when you feel depleted, you probably conserve the water in your glass by withdrawing from people. This is to protect you from running completely dry. At other times, when someone around you is sad or in need, you most likely try to cheer them up or answer their call when they reach out. You do this because you realize their glass is running empty and they need some filling.

This is so second nature to us that we even apply it when we approach God. We imagine God as having a glass, and we're the ones to properly fill it by our worship. It's like the Christmas-spirit Claus-o-meter in the movie Elf; if we have enough Christmas cheer, then the engine powers up and causes Santa's sleigh to fly. We enter a church worship experience ready to sing and do our part to fulfill God's worship "needs." If done just right, then His glass gets full, and He is able to pour blessing all over us.

This, however, is not what is taking place.

The Scripture:
"[God] is not served by human hands, as if he needed anything. Rather, he himself gives everyone life and breath and everything else."—Acts 17:25, NIV

What It Says About Worship:
God does not need anything, including our worship. He doesn't need companionship, shelter, appreciation, or bacon. He doesn't have a glass that varies between empty and

full. He doesn't have days when he feels incomplete until someone tells Him how great He is. He isn't waiting in a depleted state until Sunday morning when you and I and a billion other people gather in buildings to remind Him of His power and beauty. Nope, God doesn't need you to worship Him. He is full and complete in Himself. If He did need worship, that can be taken care of through the rocks that will worship Him if we don't (see Luke 19:40). Plus, for eternity, seraphim will fly around the throne and cry out to Him about His holiness (see Isaiah 6 and Revelation 4). In fact, "The heavens declare the glory of God; the skies proclaim the work of his hands" (Psalm 19:1, NIV). All of that takes place whether or not we decide to live lives that celebrate His glory.

So, is God needy like us? No. Does He need our worship? No. God gives us worship as a gift. We *get* to worship Him. We get to tell Him how great He is and how we are helpless without Him. It is because of His grace that we can approach Him in the first place. His glass is already full. And when we worship, our glass gets full too.

Apply It:
The next time you are in a worship service, close your eyes and see God not as one who needs your worship to complete Him, but as one who is completely full and ready to pour blessings into you. Worship because it is a privilege. To remember this, hold your hands open with your palms up as you sing and pray. This will remind you that as you give yourself completely to God, you are receiving from a God who is already complete.

My Devoted Response

Two Questions:

1. What are five things you need from God every day?

2. Even though God doesn't need our worship, what three ways are you going to worship Him today?

Week 4 - Days 6-7: Keep Worshiping!

I hope this journey has been impactful for you. My prayer is that you have discovered what worship means, you've become more energized to pursue a life of worship, and you are inspired to sing and participate fervently at church.

As today is our last day together in this devotional, I've taken the liberty to make this session a bit different from the other days. Today, with the help of leaders from our ministry at Worship Catalyst, I want to give you some next steps in your worship journey, which you can continue to use forever, as you create worship patterns, or habits, in your life.

We never "arrive" as worshipers. It's not as though one day we wake up perfectly surrendered to God in spirit and truth and stay that way from this day forward. It is a process. But as we continue, we open ourselves more and more to seeing the reality of God at work in the world and in our lives.

The more we worship, the more God uses our offering to connect us more intimately and consistently with Jesus.

Meditate on the Price Jesus Paid for You
Do this through reading again and again what Jesus did on the cross, listening to songs about His grace, and even discussing His salvation with others. The apostle Paul urged us in Romans 12:1 to respond to the mercy of God. Nothing in the world will help you worship Christ in all you do, day in and day out, more than remembering the price He paid for you on the cross.

It is to the One who shed His blood for you that you are responding.

Sing and/or Pray the Psalms
Worshipers read the Psalms a lot. Not only that, but they also pray the Psalms. Put yourself in the story, pick a psalm, and sing or read it back to God as a prayer. Many of them were written as songs and prayers anyway.

Listen to and Pray through Worship Songs
Recently I went through a three-month process where I listened only to worship songs. No country. No rock. No old-school rap. No talk radio. I was amazed by how much my heart expanded for God just by singing and praying through worship songs throughout the day as I drove. I even added worship songs to my quiet times with God. My heart softened in ways I never would have imagined, and I became a deeper and more grateful worshiper.

Pray the Names and Attributes of God
A simple google search will yield the various names of God in the Bible. If you will take the time to meditate and pray through these names, recognizing how God has revealed some of these attributes to you, you will become more aware of God's presence as you go throughout your day. For instance, Jesus is called the Great Shepherd. In what ways has God been your shepherd this week? God is sometimes called Abba (daddy, father). How has He been your dad?

Listen to Sermons from People Who Stir Your Heart
Whether it be John Piper, Tim Keller, Tony Evans, David Platt, your own pastor, or any number of other preachers, God uses gifted communicators to connect us to God and

His plan for our lives. Replace talk radio with a podcast of one of your favorite preachers and see what God might do to make you more aware of His presence throughout the day.

Be Quiet
This is really hard in today's culture. Most people are moving at light speed, accomplishing a lot but losing some of their soul along the way. Work on this discipline of being quiet before God. Get alone. Still your mind. Try to listen. Read 1 Kings 19:9-18, the story of the prophet Elijah who stood waiting to hear from God. It was in a gentle whisper that God finally spoke. It is difficult to hear God's voice, which is often still and small, when we are moving through life at a fast, loud pace.

Go on a Mission Trip
Local missions. Short-term missions. Global missions. Pick one and go! In talking with hundreds of people who have been on mission trips, here is what I have found. Every single person returns from the endeavor with two realities: They are more committed to Christ, and they have a better perspective on the life they live. You want to be more thankful? Humbler? More yielded to God? Go on a mission trip. You will come back as a stronger worshiper.

Study the Lyrics
Take the songs you are singing at your church on Sundays, or others that you really like, and look through the Bible to learn the biblical background for them. Oftentimes this will open a lot of other timeless truths that will cause you to understand more about God's character and attributes.

My Devoted Response
Find Your Meet-with-God Spot and Go There Frequently
What is the location that best helps you connect with Christ? A park? A beach? A bedroom? A boardroom? The mountains? Your backyard? Wherever that might be for you, go often. I feel most connected to God when I am near water. That could be a beach, a lake, or even the pool in my backyard. So, as often as possible, I get to a body of water and just sit. Sometimes I talk to God. Sometimes I read a book or my Bible. And sometimes I simply do and say nothing. And somehow, I am slowly restored physically, emotionally, and spiritually. Find your spot and go there as much as you can.

Talk Out Loud to God
Maybe you do this already. Unfortunately, I have talked to many people who never pray out loud. They simply think their prayers and pray internally. That isn't wrong of course. But there is something different about opening your mouth to God and speaking out loud what is on your mind, as you would a friend. When I pray in this way it keeps me focused and helps me be even more open to God somehow. There you go. Try these out. Respond to God with all your heart. Be a worshiper!

As we complete this journey, I want to thank you for the investment of your time and for the focus you have placed on worshiping God. Don't stop! Make this lifestyle of devotedly responding to God the core aspect of who you are. Enjoy God's presence. Be patient. Experiment. While I don't know how each of these practices will specifically help you connect uniquely with God, I do know that He is actively looking for those who will make the effort to approach Him with their emotions and their minds. So, worship in spirit and in truth today and always.

Austin Ryan

In Memory:
This devotional guide is offered in memory of Wes Spiegel. For the first 14 years of Worship Catalyst, he guided our Board of Directors with a steady hand and a contagious faith that continues to be his legacy. He kept us saying "yes" when we weren't sure we were ready to move forward. As for me personally, Wes was a 20-year mentor who helped me as much as anyone in my leadership journey. Everyone who knew Wes loved him, and still love his devoted wife Jayne. He was a cheerleader to many, a mentor to a select few, and a friend to all who knew him. As we, on earth, feebly try to understand and participate in worship, we know that Wes is singing bass with the seraphim on the eternal song, cheering for us as we cheer for Jesus.

Austin Ryan

Made in the USA
Monee, IL
07 April 2023